'Every page of this brilliant book ‹
passion and positivity of the author, _
where the social, emotional and mental well-being of students
is often compromised, Frederika has given us a shining light to
guide our paths as we seek to transform the educational journey
of every student we teach. *For Flourishing's Sake* offers us a fabulous
Character Education road map that teachers can confidently refer
to each and every day. Let's pop Frederika's LeAF model poster up
in every classroom and let the flourishing begin.'

– Vanessa Gamack, Mission and Education Advisor,
Anglican Schools Commission, Southern Queensland

'Frederika Roberts takes us on exciting learning journeys using
international case studies that equip us with practical strategies to
use in our education communities. All of the schools and leaders
cited in the book have one thing in common: they are on a journey to
enable staff and pupils to flourish personally and academically. You
can't help but start your own personal and professional flourishing
journey as a result.'

– Maria O'Neill, advanced skills teacher and pastoral
leader and CEO of Pastoral Support Ltd

'*For Flourishing's Sake* is a highly readable book that would be helpful
to anyone who wants to bring Positive Education into their school.
Chock full of real-life examples from all over the world, it contains
a wealth of information. *For Flourishing's Sake* is a must read and has
inspired me to grow and expand Positive Education in my school!'

– Caren Baruch-Feldman, PhD, psychologist and
author of The Grit Guide for Teens

'*For Flourishing's Sake* asks us why we wanted to be teachers. I'm hopeful that Positive Education has the potential to embed learning and happiness at the heart of all educational organisations: that's why I became a teacher. Do read and put the principles of Positive Education into practice so that everyone working in education really does flourish and, for all our sakes, our future citizens both learn and are happy.'

– Vivienne Porritt, leadership consultant, Co-founder and Strategic Leader of #WomenEd, Vice President of Chartered College of Teaching

'If you want to know how to implement Positive Education in your school, this is the right book. Frederika's natural and comprehensive way of showcasing practical tools bridges the gap between research and practice. This is exactly the kind of knowledge-based and educationally reflecting support that school leaders, students and parents need.'

– Gilda Scarfe, CEO and Founder of Positive Ed

'What a joy to read! For anyone who thinks we have lost our way in education in recent times you only have to read Frederika's fantastic analysis of schools and school leaders whose approach to creating a climate of Positive Education, coupled with a focus on character and a passion for the curriculum can allow children not only to grow, but to flourish! Delighted to see the brilliant work of CMAT's Claire Probert at Lancot Challenger Academy showcased alongside so many other talented educators in this amazing book.'

– Stephen Chamberlain, Chief Executive Officer of Active Learning Trust and National Leader of Governance, Former CEO, Challenger Multi-Academy Trust

FOR FLOURISHING'S SAKE

by the same author

Character Toolkit for Teachers
100+ Classroom and Whole School Character
Education Activities for 5- to 11-Year-Olds
Frederika Roberts and Elizabeth Wright
Foreword by Kristján Kristjánsson
ISBN 978 1 78592 490 3
eISBN 978 1 78450 879 1

Character Toolkit Strength Cards
Frederika Roberts and Elizabeth Wright
ISBN 978 1 78775 273 3

of related interest

The Mental Health and Wellbeing Handbook for Schools
Transforming Mental Health Support on a Budget
Clare Erasmus
ISBN 978 1 78592 481 1
eISBN 978 1 78450 869 2

How to Transform Your School into an LGBT+ Friendly Place
A Practical Guide for Nursery, Primary and Secondary Teachers
Dr Elly Barnes MBE and Dr Anna Carlile
ISBN 978 1 78592 349 4
eISBN 978 1 78450 684 1

How to Be a Peaceful School
Practical Ideas, Stories and Inspiration
Edited by Anna Lubelska
ISBN 978 1 78592 156 8
eISBN 978 1 78450 424 3

FOR FLOURISHING'S SAKE

Using Positive Education to Support Character Development and Well-being

FREDERIKA ROBERTS

Foreword by Andrew Cowley

Jessica Kingsley Publishers
London and Philadelphia

First published in 2020
by Jessica Kingsley Publishers
73 Collier Street
London N1 9BE, UK

www.jkp.com

Library of Congress Cataloging in Publication Data
A CIP catalog record for this book is available from the Library of Congress

British Library Cataloguing in Publication Data
A CIP catalogue record for this book is available from the British Library

ISBN 978 1 78775 024 1
eISBN 978 1 78775 025 8

Printed and bound in Great Britain

To Simon, Charlie and Hannah (aka Babychick/Banban).

You are my world.

Contents

Foreword

If we believe everything we see and hear on mainstream or social media, we live in a time of despair and a lack of hope. The uncertainty, of our relationship and status within Europe and with the rest of the world, politicians of all sides shouting at each other in Parliament or on television, 'celebrities' using their 'status' to promote some product or more likely themselves and always those people who pop up with a problem to every solution; these, and a combination of other elements, could leave us with an extremely negative view of life in the 21st century.

Where is the positivity that our young people, in particular, need to guide them through the journey, challenges and obstacles of modern life?

This work by Frederika Roberts may just be the beacon, for educators and their young charges, that lights the way. Fred, as she is known to her friends and loved ones, makes a powerful argument for positive virtues and values.

For Flourishing's Sake sets the case for Positive Education, drawing upon the links with Character Education, values and well-being that make the pastoral part of our role, the 'hidden curriculum' as it were, so vital in the lives of our pupils and students. You will come away from Fred's work with a deep sense that positive and pastoral education underpins, rather than undermines, the academic curriculum.

Building from her deep-seated belief in the values of fairness and social justice, Fred takes us on a truly international journey from Australia to Iceland, via Finland, Lichfield and three contrasting settings within the London Borough of Bexley, drawing on the practical advice of seasoned yet impassioned practitioners. Fred's work is also soundly grounded in research too, particularly in relation to the much lauded Finnish system of education, giving the reader far more insight than the mere soundbite of social media might provide.

Everything in Fred's work draws back to her LeAF (Learn and Flourish) model which clearly sets out how all the elements of well-being, values, achievement, community and strong, visible leadership feed and support the model of Positive Education. Positive Education isn't a mere bolt-on, another task for weary schools and teachers to take on; at its heart are strong and effective relationships and an authentic desire to make our young learners responsible and reliable citizens of the future.

What struck me most about *For Flourishing's Sake* is the universality of the values and scope of Positive Education, from an international and societal perspective. Lichfield Cathedral School, Townley Grammar School and Lessness Heath Primary School could not be any more different in their catchment areas and the socio-economic profile of their intakes, yet you will see the core principles apply to each to support their students and staff.

Frederika Roberts brings the same blunt honesty to her writing as she does to her speaking and those who have had the pleasure to meet her will know and appreciate the warmth and genuine desire to make a difference that *For Flourishing's Sake* sets out to make.

Andrew Cowley

Andrew Cowley is the author of *The Wellbeing Toolkit* (Bloomsbury Education, 2019), deputy headteacher of a primary school in South London, and co-founder of the Healthy Toolkit twitter account (@HealthyToolkit) and blog.

www.healthyteachertoolkit.wordpress.com

Acknowledgements

The physical act of writing a book is only part of the story; it cannot happen without immense and sustained support and encouragement from numerous people. The first people I'd like to acknowledge and thank are those whose generous contributions have brought Positive Education to life on the pages you are about to read.

Carrying out the interviews – then reading back through my copious notes and listening back to the recordings to pull out key stories and insights – made me feel immensely optimistic. I only hope I have been able to do justice to the amazing contributions so that you, too, will feel that same sense of hope, excitement and inspiration when you read them. I would therefore like to express my heartfelt thanks to:[1]

- Flora Barton, Headteacher, Crowmarsh Gifford Church of England Primary School, UK

- Adele Bates, Behaviour and Education Specialist, UK

- Paul Bateson, Teacher, UK

- Rebecca Comizio, School Psychologist, New Canaan Country School, USA

---

1   Please note that it is the nature of the writing and publishing cycle that by the time a book is published, people may have moved on from their roles at the time I interviewed them. The organizations they are associated with and the approaches adopted by those organizations were correct at the time of writing.

- Fabian de Fabiani, Director of Character Education and Well-Being, Odyssey Trust for Education and Assistant Headteacher, Townley Grammar School, UK

- Kti Dossot, Founder, KtiD – Vision to Value, France

- Eleanor Ellis Bryant, Subject Leader for Religious Studies and Staff Governor, University of Birmingham School, UK

- Serdar Ferit, Co-CEO, Lyfta, Finland and UK

- Ian Flintoff, Director, Affirm Consulting, UK

- Julie Goldstein, Principal, Breakthrough Magnet School South, USA

- Dóra Guðrún Guðmundsdóttir, Division Head, Determinants of Health Division, Directorate of Health, Iceland

- Kelly Hannaghan, Well-Being Leader, Lessness Heath Primary School, UK

- Gary Lewis, Headteacher, Kings Langley School, UK

- Katrina Mankani, Director of Positive Education, Sunmarke School and Regent International School, Dubai

- Rhiannon McGee, Head of Positive Education, Geelong Grammar School, Australia

- Dan Morrow, CEO, Woodland Academy Trust, UK

- Katy O'Connor, Headteacher, Lessness Heath Primary School, UK

- Patrick Ottley-O'Connor, Education Consultant, Leadership Coach and Headteacher, Executive Principal, North Liverpool Academy, UK

- Jo Owens, Director of Ethical Leadership, Lichfield Cathedral School, UK

- Elke Paul, Positive Education Consultant and Head of Positive Education, Berlin Brandenburg International School, Germany

- Claire Probert, Headteacher, Lancot Challenger Academy, UK

- Anni Silverdale Poole, Director, HLS for Whole School Well-Being, and author of *Simply Being YOU*, UK

- Rebecca Tigue, Head of School, University of Birmingham School, UK.

This book would not exist without a publisher, so I would also like to express my immense gratitude to the entire team at Jessica Kingsley Publishers, and especially to my wonderful editor James Cherry. He 'got it' when I excitedly phoned him from my hotel in Paris at the end of one of the modules on my Master of Applied Positive Psychology course at Anglia Ruskin University to tell him about my idea. He championed this book from that first moment, helping me refine my proposal so that the rest of the editorial team would share my vision. He then put his trust in me, even when my timescales became a little 'tight' (to say the least!), to deliver the book I'd promised, on time. During the planning, writing and editing process, James offered his usual wisdom and insights to help me make this book the best it can be. James epitomizes everything an editor should be. This is the third project I have had the pleasure of working with him on and I look forward to many more in the future.

On the subject of my Master's degree and the module – Appreciative Inquiry – that gave me the idea for this book, I'd like to thank the formidable Jean-Christophe Barralis, co-tutor on that module, for introducing me to Kti Dossot. I also hugely appreciate the support of my Positive Education module tutor and dissertation supervisor Dr Ilona Boniwell, whose feedback helped me refine the 'LeAF' model of Positive Education I have used as a basis for the structure of this book. Her insights and support were invaluable – without the groundwork that went into researching and developing the 'LeAF' model, this book would have been much harder to write! This degree has given me so much more than a qualification and insights to support my writing and my school-based work, however; it has enriched my life with amazing, inspirational people I am fortunate enough to call my friends. In particular, I have valued the support of my closest group of 'MAPPsters' – the group we affectionately call 'PP Islanders'; these wonderful friends have inspired, supported and cheered me on with an unconditional love that moves me to tears! On a practical note, I'd like to particularly thank 'PP Islander' Sara Hlín Hálfdanardóttir for introducing me to Dóra Guðrún Guðmundsdóttir.

I am also immensely grateful to Andrew Cowley for taking the time to write such a beautiful and thoughtful foreword for this book. As a busy school leader and teacher, author and co-founder of Healthy Toolkit, not to mention in-demand speaker at educational conferences and other events, I hugely appreciate him taking the time to read my manuscript and provide his thoughts and insights.

My gratitude also goes to my friend and former business partner Elizabeth Wright. The work we have done together has helped me immensely in developing a wonderful network of contacts to approach as contributors for this book, but beyond that, I am deeply thankful for her encouragement and unwavering belief in me, especially at times when inevitable self-doubt crept in. In this respect, I have also had fantastic support from my wonderful coach, Leoni Kitchin; she helped me 'get my mojo back' when I most needed it, which helped immensely when writing this book!

To everyone in my professional and personal life who, for longer than I can remember, has had to endure me being a 'book-bore', rambling on endlessly about 'whole school Positive Education', along with my stock response of 'I'll deal with this once I've finished writing': Thank you for your patience, and I hope you'll feel it was worth it! More than anyone, this applies to my husband Simon and our daughters Charlie and Hannah, who suffered me being present in body but not in spirit for far too long, but did so with grace, patience, understanding and so much love, support and encouragement. Thank you for all that you do and all that you enable me to do. I love and appreciate you more than words will ever be able to express!

Finally, I would like to thank you, dear reader, for picking up this book; thank you for caring, for wanting to make a difference, for being hopeful and for putting your trust in me by reading this book as a stepping stone towards making education better.

INTRODUCTION

We're doing our part in enabling the kids to become the future we need them to be.

Julie Goldstein

What are Positive and Character Education?

Why did you become a teacher? Before all your training and experience, before you began taking on more responsibilities, before you had to concern yourself with policies, inspections, frameworks and curricula, what was your motivation?

Most teachers I know – and that included me before stress curtailed my teaching career – wanted to make a difference in children's lives, to set them up for a happy and successful future, to equip them for adult life. Most teachers I know still have the same goal many years into their teaching careers. Wanting to make a difference to children's lives is cited by the Education Support Partnership (2018) as the main reason teachers love working in education.

What do parents want for their children? Seligman *et al.* (2009) say the answer is well-being. Yet, they point out, schools teach children about achievement; they are oriented (mostly) purely towards the academic. Well-being and academic achievement, however, are not mutually exclusive. Seligman *et al.* call this '*Positive Education*'. The term was coined when Seligman was invited to help Geelong Grammar School (see 'Spotlight 1') in Australia develop their whole school well-being provision. The school's fascinating journey is described in detail in Norrish's (2015) book, *Positive Education: The Geelong Grammar School Journey*.

Character Education, according to the Jubilee Centre for Character and Virtues (2017), encompasses all activities of an educational nature that contribute to the development of a child's virtues; character is essentially our moral compass. The Positive Psychology approach to character is strengths-based; its foundations are the 24 VIA character strengths we all share.[1]

Research evidence supports that Character and Positive Education improve academic outcomes (Adler 2016; Berkowitz and Bier 2005), so even from a purely academic perspective it makes sense to look at education through this broader lens and focus on well-being alongside academic outcomes.

Are 'Character Education' and 'Positive Education' interchangeable terms?

The International Positive Education Network (IPEN) defines Positive Education with the 'double helix'[2] of 'academics' and 'character & well-being'. The Jubilee Centre refers to flourishing as the 'ultimate aim of character education' (2017, p.1); flourishing is also referred to extensively in Positive Psychology. Character and Positive Education are not identical, but each includes elements of the other, and both have the aim of promoting flourishing. I see Character Education as a component of Positive Education, but in the interest of simplicity, I will use the two terms interchangeably in this book.

It's worth noting that some countries favour one term over the other. 'Character Education' is well recognized in the USA and the UK. Schools in Portugal, on the other hand, have moved away from the term due to the moral aspects associated with it, as well as its association with the country's history of dictatorship from the 1920s to the 1970s, which had Character Education at its ideology's core (Lopes *et al.* 2013). In Australia, the birthplace of the term 'Positive Education', this is the one most commonly used.

---

1   www.viacharacter.org/character-strengths
2   www.positiveeducation.net

How will this book help you?

If you have picked up this book, it's likely you are interested in exploring ways to introduce, enhance or expand Positive Education in your school. To support you in your endeavours, this book will combine research evidence, policy and case-study examples from various countries.

I hope the case studies will provide you with inspiration through real-life examples of the impact of whole school Positive Education. I will include a little bit of background information about each school or person featured in this book in the chapter in which I mention it/them for the first time.

On days when you think 'This can't be done', or 'We don't have the time/budget/resources/energy…', it is my hope that this book will be your friendly companion, giving you the inspiration and encouragement you need, along with a healthy dose of practical ideas to support you in improving education.

A few words about the themes and case studies

I have had the privilege of interviewing many wonderful contributors to this book; the majority of these were headteachers/principals, but I spoke to a variety of education and well-being professionals – including the head of a government division – involved in well-being initiatives in schools and higher-education institutions. I interviewed people working in, or having researched the education systems of, the UK, USA, Australia, Finland, Iceland, France, Germany and Dubai. I therefore hope that, wherever you are based, you will find some nuggets of inspiration and practical ideas you can apply in your own setting. As Chapter 2 will show, Positive Education is not a 'one size fits all' solution, but with sensitivity to, and awareness of, each school's and country's unique cultural context, it can be implemented anywhere.

My aim is for this book to provide you with an element of inspiration and emotional lift through the stories that make teachers and school leaders feel joy and elation when they think about their school's Positive Education journey and achievements (see Chapter 13).

To this end, wherever possible, I used a four-step questioning technique adapted from the four 'foundational questions' of Appreciative Inquiry (Cooperrider, Whitney and Stavros 2003, pp.23–24) to encourage my interviewees to:

- tell me a story relating to their experience of Positive Education, focusing on what most energized and inspired them

- reflect upon and describe what strengths they and/or their school community used in the story

- share how the experience they described in the story made them feel

- dream about the future – for their school and education overall.

I then extracted the themes which form the chapter structure of this book and which are linked to the elements of my 'LeAF' model.

'LeAF' stands for 'learn and flourish'. This sums up my view on the purpose of education, which reflects the definitions of Positive Education and Character Education outlined earlier.

LeAF is a model I began to develop as part of an assignment (Roberts 2018) for the Positive Education module of my MSc in Applied Positive Psychology at Anglia Ruskin University, UK, and developed further in my final dissertation (Roberts 2019). I analyzed existing models of Positive Education around the world, then attempted to plug any gaps in existing models and frameworks to create a comprehensive updated model. In the visual model (Figure 1.1), the leaves represent the structural elements that form whole school Positive Education (see Chapters 2–12) plus the aims of Positive Education (see Chapter 1). The trunk represents 'evaluation', which I cover in Chapter 4. The roots underpin all the Positive Education work done in school and are derived from the body of Positive Psychology and Character Education research and literature (see Appendix). Government policy is represented as the soil on which the tree grows. In Chapters 1 and 4, I highlight how and why schools need to consider the steps they can take to influence education policy.

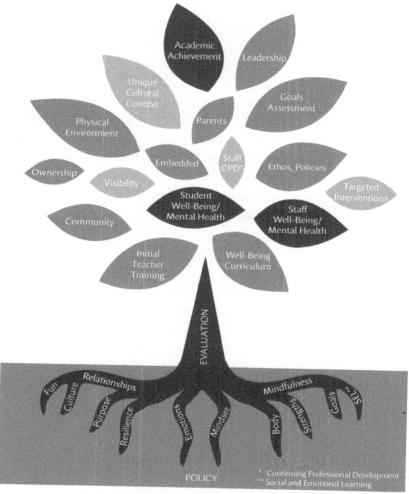

*Figure I.1. The LeAF (learn and flourish) model
of whole school Positive Education*
(Roberts 2019)

How to read this book

You can, of course, pick this book up and read it from cover to cover. I ordered the chapters in a way that I hope will allow the themes to flow from broad foundational principles to more specific aspects of whole school Positive Education. If, however, you're short on time, you can dip in and out to read about specific aspects of Positive Education.

I have included two extended case studies (Australia's Geelong Grammar School and the UK's Lancot Challenger Academy, 'Spotlights' 1 and 2) for the following reasons: Geelong Grammar was the school where the term 'Positive Education' was first coined, and Lancot has an unusual approach to curriculum design and delivery. Additionally, I have included a chapter ('Spotlight 3') that highlights how national policy and international co-operation can support whole school Positive Education.

Over to you!

However you choose to read this book, please don't just read it and then let it gather dust on a bookshelf. Take action! You don't have to tackle everything at once, but do something to introduce or increase the focus on well-being and character in your school. Look at everything you do through the lens of Positive Education to help your students, your staff/colleagues (and you!), and the wider school community, flourish!

Chapter 1

AIMS OF POSITIVE EDUCATION

I want children to find their purpose.

Claire Probert

Education vs Positive Education

In an ideal world, promoting well-being would be intrinsic to education (see also Chapter 10). When I spoke to Adele Bates, a behaviour and education specialist[1] who spent a month in Finland in early 2019 to learn about the Finnish education system, she told me something that made my heart sing; she asked every single adult she met in Finnish schools: 'When students leave your school, if you have done your job well, what does success look like?' All their answers (Bates 2019) were along the following lines (see also the video on her blog):

- They will be happy and have the confidence to follow their interests and dreams.

- Co-operation with others will be one of their key skills.

---

1   www.adelebateseducation.co.uk

- They will have the ability to learn. On this point, some of the people she asked elaborated further and talked about the importance of preparing children for the ability to adapt to a future we cannot predict, with jobs we don't know will exist. Others said that the world is full of conflict and we need to prepare children to create positive change.

In Finland, character and well-being are built into the entire ethos for education. How do we achieve this in all schools, in all countries? We don't live in an ideal world, so for now at least, we need to be more explicit about our aims and our practices; we need to be more deliberate about including Positive Psychology and Character Education in our everyday school lives until it becomes integral to everything we do.

Think back to the question I asked at the start of the Introduction: Why did you become a teacher? Where did the fire in your belly come from? Did you dream of helping children flourish? The great news is you're already doing so much more than you might realize! As a teacher, every day you help children navigate the challenges of growing up, of feeling frustrated by the process of learning, of adolescent hormonal swings; you're helping them deal with emotions, recognize their strengths, discover and be comfortable with who they are while working to grow into the best person they can be. That is Positive Education! When your school's behaviour reward and sanctions system teaches children about consequences for their actions, when you ask children to manage their time so they can work and rest, you are teaching them about self-regulation. That's Character Education! You don't need to re-invent the wheel and you don't need to beat yourself up about not doing enough. You simply need to look at what you're already doing through the lens of Positive Education, and build on that.

Reaching for the stars

Positive Education is often described in terms that combine pedagogy, Positive Psychology (including character strengths) and academic achievement. Seligman *et al.*'s (2009) definition combines teaching children to develop the skills for academic success and for happiness. Positive Education is also described as preventing mental health issues from arising or worsening, and promoting happiness and well-being, commonly described in Positive Psychology as *flourishing*. Boniwell's 'two pillars' (2018) of Positive Education – resilience and well-being – each include aspects of prevention and promotion. Weare (2015) writes about promoting well-being for everyone and brings up the need for preventative and restorative targeted interventions (see Chapter 11). By building adolescents' resilience in educational establishments, the UPRIGHT[2] programme (see 'Spotlight 3') aims to promote mental well-being and prevent mental illness. White and Murray's (2015) definition of Positive Education includes promotion, prevention and Character Education.

A whole school approach

The need for a whole school approach has been documented in numerous reports and research papers (Jubilee Centre 2017; Public Health England 2014; Stirling and Emery 2016; Waters 2011; Waters *et al.* 2015). White (2016) stresses the importance of school culture and Weare (2015) mentions that when robust programmes or interventions are integral to every aspect of school life, there is strong potential for a positive impact on well-being and the reduction of mental health issues. The *Health Promoting Schools* programme in Iceland (see 'Spotlight 3') adopts a whole school and local community approach.

Katrina Mankani, Director of Positive Education at Fortes Education, told me that Positive Education should never be just a curriculum, but rather a whole school approach is needed. She explained how, for example, this looks when giving children feedback: Do we praise the steps they have taken, thereby boosting their character development, or do we praise their intelligence? Teachers need to be trained in this, of course, to ensure consistency.

---

2   http://uprightproject.eu

Two private schools in Dubai

Fortes Education, in Dubai, consists of Sunmarke School and Regent International School. Sunmarke School takes children from nursery through to 18 years old. Regent International School is a primary school covering Kindergarten/Early Years to age 11.

Regent International School was established in 1992 and included a values system similar to Character Education, which wasn't initially empirically based, until the founders discovered the work of Martin Seligman and IPEN.[3] In September 2016 they brought in trainers from Geelong Grammar School in Australia (see 'Spotlight 1') to train their teachers and those from the brand-new Sunmarke School, which opened its doors from day one as a Positive Education school.

In addition to all their teachers being trained by Geelong staff, the leadership team implemented Positive Education across three tiers: organizational tier (ensuring their policies were consistent and fit for purpose), pro-active tier (explicit and implicit well-being teaching, see Chapters 9 and 10) and responsive tier (targeted interventions, see Chapter 11).

A secondary 'free school' in the UK

The University of Birmingham (UoB) School is a *free school*[4] in Birmingham, UK, created in response to the government asking universities whether they wanted to set up their own schools to help research extend outside the boundaries of academia, professionalize teaching and give the profession more recognition. Professor James Arthur, who was Head of the School of Education at the University of Birmingham and was setting up its Jubilee Centre for Character and Virtues, was instrumental in working with others from the university to set up UoB school. The school was designed to serve the city of Birmingham. It draws in students from four distinct 'nodes' across the city, agreed with the city council based on where

---

3   www.positiveeducation.net
4   In the UK, a 'free school' is funded by the government but falls outside the remit of the local education authority's control. It is set up by a group of individuals or an organization; in this case the University of Birmingham.

there was the highest need for school places and/or the lowest social mobility. The aim was to create a diverse and inclusive school community for the city and to give Character Education the same weight as academic success. From the outset, the vision was to build a school that would create better citizens and allow its staff, pupils and community to flourish.

UoB School opened its doors in September 2015. It is the UK's first secondary University Training School, allowing trainee teachers and practising teachers to benefit from the unique links between the research of the University of Birmingham's School of Education and other academic departments, and the practical everyday school environment.

School transformation through a whole school Positive Education approach

Lessness Heath Primary School, a school in a deprived area in Kent (UK), did not start out as a Positive Education or Character Education school. Its Headteacher, Katy O'Connor, told me that it was 'a very dark place to be' when she joined in Autumn 2015 after The Primary First Trust took over the school. It was a school with severe issues around teaching and learning, angry parents, low attendance, poor behaviour, a neglected infrastructure, low staff morale, high staff turnover and long-term sickness absences. Katy took the initial brave steps of not focusing on teaching and learning or outcomes, but on rebuilding relationships to create a 'community that did something special for children'.

She brought in Kelly Hannaghan, initially on a self-employed part-time basis, but Kelly's time spent in school rapidly increased from one to five days per week and, since September 2017, she has been employed as a full-time well-being leader in the school. By driving a big push on building relationships and trust within the school community, and taking a whole school perspective on Positive Education, Katy and Kelly have changed the school's entire culture. Lessness Heath Primary School is a state-funded school just outside Greater London, so it does not receive the enhanced funding that London schools are entitled to. The changes achieved in this school were achieved on the same tight budget that many schools in the UK and around the world face.

> Well-being needs to be looked at by every school.
>
> Kelly Hannaghan

Crowmarsh Gifford Primary School is a Church of England School[5] in rural Oxfordshire (UK) educating children from age 4 to 11. As a small school with relatively low numbers of pupils requiring additional educational or financial support, Crowmarsh Gifford does not have recourse to large amounts of additional funding and is therefore another great example of how culture change and whole school Positive Education can be achieved without the need for vast financial resources.

When Headteacher Flora Barton took up her post five years ago, she brought in Diana Pardoe (see Further Reading), who introduced a process called 'Purple Learning'. This started off as a way to introduce staff and children to the characteristics needed for effective learning, but soon broadened out into all aspects of the children's and teachers' lives.

> The whole ethos Purple Learning has brought to the school has absolutely transformed the way we, as staff, and the children look at learning.
>
> Flora Barton

Social justice, not social mobility

When I read the 'Welcome from the CEO'[6] on the UK's Woodland Academy Trust's website, I cried. I cried because, on seeing Dan Morrow's passion and sense of purpose so unapologetically displayed as a rallying cry for change, my emotions of gratitude and hope overwhelmed me. When I interviewed Dan, I felt goose bumps as I heard his passion and fierce determination to make education

---

5   As a Church of England school, they uphold Christian values and observe daily collective worship, but they are state-funded through the local education authority.

6   www.woodlandacademytrust.co.uk/our-trust/welcome-from-the-ceo

better. He summed up Positive Education with his ethos: 'How does this school fulfil dreams?' I will elaborate on Dan's incredible personal story in Chapter 5, but for now, I'll share what he said to me in our first conversation:

> I'm not interested in producing a generation of capitalist automatons. I'm interested in producing a generation of social justice champions...
>
> We don't talk about social mobility; we talk about social justice. We should always be challenging the system to be better for the learners and not accept working in an unfair and unjust system. We do, but we don't stop there.

Dan Morrow

Three key aims of Positive Education

The three fundamental aims of Positive Education are: student well-being/mental health,[7] staff well-being/mental health, and academic achievement. These are represented by three of the leaves on the LeAF model (see Figure 1.1 in the Introduction), and every theme explored in this book contributes to one or more of these aims.

Student well-being

You've probably read the distressing statistics: Of all recorded cases of adult mental illness worldwide, half start in adolescence (Patel *et al.* 2007). In the UK, one in ten children is diagnosed with a behavioural/emotional or mental health issue, and youth suicide is one of the main causes of death in young people (Weare 2015). A quarter of adolescents in Australia have mental health issues, and children as young as 4 years old receive mental health diagnoses (Waters 2017).

While students who are mentally well generally enjoy better relationships in adolescence and later life, have better physical

---

7   This includes character strengths/character development.

health, are more optimistic, achieve more academically, face better employment and higher earnings prospects and are more likely to be engaged in their community as adults (Waters 2017), there are strong links between mental health issues and poor educational outcomes, as well as concerns related to excessive risk-taking and drugs. When children develop their self-esteem, their social skills and their problem-solving abilities, however, these can protect them against mental illness (Patel *et al.* 2007).

Schools are uniquely placed to help children learn the skills that can shield them from mental illness in later life and give them the chance to lead their best possible life. According to Konu and Rimpelä (2002), broad preventative initiatives are crucial because schools are the principal setting to promote health in young people. This view is also supported by Stirling and Emery (2016), who stress that mental health is important for all children and therefore schools need to introduce ways to have a positive impact on every child's well-being.

The ethos of Townley Grammar and King Henry Schools in Kent in the UK is highly focused on providing their students with every opportunity to flourish. Townley Grammar School is an 11–18 state-funded academically selective girls' school, where Character Education has been systematically introduced and developed over the past few years with the aim of promoting social mobility. Fabian de Fabiani, Assistant Headteacher at Townley Grammar and Director of Character Education and well-being for the Odyssey Trust, told me that he sees these as closely linked. In addition to a robust Character Education and leadership programme for pupils, the school has a wide range of student well-being initiatives, including well-being ambassadors, peer-to-peer support, 'Mental Health First Aid',[8] coaching and mindfulness training, expert support from counsellors, and a therapy dog. Much of the school's Character Education and well-being work is based on Seligman's (2012) PERMA[9] model for flourishing. In line with the school's

---

8   https://mhfaengland.org
9   PERMA: Positive Emotion, Engagement, Relationships, Meaning, Accomplishments.

value system, when the opportunity arose to create a Multi-Academy Trust[10] and extend the Character Education provision and values-driven culture to a school that was rated as 'requiring improvement', the Odyssey Trust for Education was formed and an 11–18 state-funded school, King Henry School, was brought into the newly formed Trust. Their Character Education journey is now underway.

A focus on well-being and relationships is also at the core of Lessness Heath Primary School's ethos. As Kelly Hannaghan told me, they want to 'create a situation where children are life ready'. Their whole school approach includes dedicated time on well-being activities, such as holding two well-being days in January that are off-timetable for all pupils.

In Finland, according to Adele Bates, teachers have the 'time, space and flexibility to consider the whole child' (Bates 2019). This includes reducing a child's workload while they are dealing with difficulties at home, for example.

Situated in central England, Lichfield Cathedral School is a small but growing independent academically non-selective school for boys and girls from early years to 18. It is steeped in Christian values with a rich history dating back approximately 800 years, and has existed in its current form since 1942. The culture there, led from the top, is to consider the whole child. Jo Owens, Director of Ethical Leadership, told me that the headteacher refers to 'glorious individuals'.

Staff well-being

In order for my children to flourish, my staff need to flourish.

Dan Morrow

---

10 An academy in England is a school funded by the government but run independently. At the time of writing, around three-quarters of English secondary schools are academies. Because they are not controlled by the local education authority, they are able to set their own curriculum, holiday dates, etc. A Multi-Academy Trust is a group of academies that work closely with each other and have some common governance, usually with a common Chief Executive Officer and governing board.

Everything has to begin with the staff. If your staff are happy and thriving, this will be reflected in the children. If their teachers are passionate, engaged and excited every morning, the children will be as well.

Flora Barton

Although students are absolutely central and the reason we do what we do, to put them first, you have to have staff in the best possible condition.

Patrick Ottley-O'Connor

Patrick Ottley-O'Connor is an education consultant, leadership coach and headteacher who steps into leadership roles in schools that require support. He is currently Executive Headteacher at North Liverpool Academy in the UK. Patrick has over 15 years' experience as a headteacher; from day one in any new school, he communicates a clear message that staff need to look after themselves first. He sees this as critical to any school improvement. He says this is counter-intuitive for many in education as it's such a caring profession that 'we become selfless; but rather than be selfless in our actions for the children, we need to be selfish first of all'. In a previous school, he managed to save significant amounts of money by making difficult decisions such as making class sizes slightly bigger, but then invested the savings into projects that made a huge difference. Whenever he asks staff what they want, invariably they say they want time to do their job – cutting out waste on bureaucracy – and the building they work in needs to be fit for purpose. In this particular school, they had beautiful buildings, but there was a big open space housing the language lab, so Patrick invested almost £150,000 of the money they'd saved, 'putting walls up to create spaces'. Staff supported Patrick's cost-saving decisions as they understood these were needed so that every teacher would have a minimum of 20 percent 'PPA' (planning, preparation and assessment) time.

Kelly Hannaghan told me that at Lessness Heath Primary School, they see staff well-being as essential to securing their children's futures. All staff are taught well-being strategies. Stirling and Emery

(2016) present evidence suggesting that children's well-being and the school climate overall is improved when staff well-being improves, yet the data around staff well-being in schools is as depressing as the statistics on children's mental health.

> Given that I have highly trained, highly competent people, what circumstances are stopping them from flourishing?
>
> Dan Morrow

The National Union of Teachers[11] gathered data on teacher stress in 2013, which showed that over 80 percent of teachers suffer from anxiety, depression or stress related to their work, and that, according to the Health and Safety Executive (HSE), they are amongst the most stressed workers in Britain. They cited HSE findings showing that anxiety, depression and stress resulted in a loss of close to 14 million working days nationally. The numbers of teachers leaving the profession are increasing, as are, worryingly, teacher suicide rates. More recent figures from the Education Support Partnership (2018) showed that 67 percent of education professionals (80% of senior leaders) report being stressed, nearly three-quarters struggle to relax after work and view their work/life balance as negative, and 75 percent experience work-related mental health issues. According to these figures, nearly 60 percent of teachers have considered leaving the profession because of the pressure it exerts on their well-being. Three-quarters of them name excessive workload as the main reason. The Education Support Partnership (2018) recommends that schools' well-being provision should include staff activities, and that staff well-being should be assessed in schools.

> Children see teachers who are stressed, teachers who leave for long periods of sickness, teachers who just come in every day exhausted, and they pick up on this.
>
> Flora Barton

---

11 The National Union of Teachers (now the National Education Union after an amalgamation with the Association of Teachers and Lecturers) is the largest education union in Europe. For more details, visit www.neu.org.uk

Teaching is not an easy job and comes with many in-built stressors. As Katrina Mankani said, 'it's like presenting to the board seven times a day'! Kelly Hannaghan told me that the role of teachers in a school like Lessness Heath Primary, where lots of children have extreme emotional needs, takes its toll at times. She described the role of teachers as almost parent-like, as teachers become the children's attachment figures. But schools and their leadership teams can do much to mitigate the stresses of teaching by focusing on teacher well-being.

In Finland, Adele Bates noticed that teachers have a high level of autonomy and trust, which impacts positively on their workload and stress levels. In her third of three blogs on education in Finland, Adele Bates (2019) outlines some key elements of the Finnish education system that contribute to staff well-being, such as low contact/teaching hours (18–23), no government inspection body or league tables, the choice of content and methodology in teaching, no performance-related pay, extensive well-paid parental leave, and encouragement to take sabbaticals.

A policy focus on staff well-being does not need to originate at government/national level, however. At Lessness Heath Primary School, for example, the leadership team ensures that staff feel empowered. Headteacher Katy O'Connor told me that when she joined the school, staff turnover was very high and she struggled to recruit new teachers because of the Ofsted[12] label of 'requiring improvement' and because, despite the high cost of living associated with being situated on the outskirts of London, the staff pay-scales do not provide staff with inner-London salaries. After three years as a headteacher at the school, her staff levels are now stable.

She gave me the example of a staff member overwhelmed by workload and other pressures despite Katy having already done extensive work on changing the school's culture, including introducing a marking policy to reduce teacher workload. Kelly and Katy had a number of open conversations that helped this person

---

12 Ofsted is the Office for Standards in Education in England. It is the government's schools inspection body.

shift their perspective and go from the point of resignation to supporting other staff with their challenges.

The workload issues caused by marking were also a major concern for Flora Barton when she took up her post as Headteacher at Crowmarsh Gifford Primary School. In one of her first staff meetings, she told them they would strive towards ensuring 'everyone could leave at least twice a week at 4.15pm with nothing in their hands'. She wanted staff to enjoy life outside of school. Five years later, Flora's Year 6 (age 10–11) teacher has not taken any pupil books home to mark in almost three years because he gives verbal feedback in lessons. Every teacher in the school, including Flora, now leaves at least twice a week at 4.15pm 'with nothing in their hands'. The focus on staff well-being goes beyond marking; with anything she does in school, Flora and her leadership team ask themselves how this will impact on staff workload.

> Well-being isn't just about the kids, it's also about the staff. We've been able to achieve some quite amazing things because of making sure that well-being is always at the heart of everything we do.
>
> Flora Barton

Another teacher at Lessness Heath Primary suffered a personal tragedy which required her to take time off work. Because of the school's well-being policy and the ability to have open discussions around mental health, she was able to eventually return to work part-time and is now flourishing.

Policy changes focusing on staff well-being have had a positive impact at Lichfield Cathedral School, too. Because of the school's organic growth, the school has a quirky structure spread out across several buildings around Lichfield Cathedral and a separate site. This physical feature of the school resulted in staff sending and receiving many internal e-mails. The school's leadership team therefore made a decision to set an e-mail curfew between 7pm and 7am, legitimizing staff not to respond to e-mails immediately. This has made a big difference in giving staff permission to go home and stop working in the evenings. Key to the effectiveness of this policy has been the effort by members of the senior leadership team not to e-mail staff during the curfew hours. If people do send an e-mail after curfew, it's either a mistake or an emergency, so this is rare. Staff still respond to e-mails within 24 hours (or on a Monday if they receive an e-mail over the weekend), so are still accessible to parents. They now also set automated out of office e-mail responders, removing the pressure to reply when they are not at work. In conjunction with the e-mail curfew, the school now has a policy not to duplicate tasks, so if something can be dealt with by e-mail, there is no need to also hold a meeting.

Eleanor Ellis Bryant, Subject Leader for Religious Studies at UoB School, told me of some of the ways that the school focuses on teacher well-being: The school week has been reorganized so that meetings and Continuing Professional Development (CPD) take place during school hours rather than after school. The school and its governors have committed to providing staff with ten in-service training days per year. Through the student enrichment programme, teachers have the opportunity to pursue their own passions while getting to know students better in an informal setting. Work at UoB school, according to Eleanor, is very challenging. The school pushes their teachers hard, but 'you are a person, not a tool to get percentages out of children'.

Townley Grammar School has staff well-being champions, and staff receive well-being CPD sessions. Fabian de Fabiani mentioned the impact of PERMA (Seligman 2012) training:

> With teachers who had received PERMA training about 'purpose', we found that when you have a strong sense of purpose, you can see the ultimate goal, so well-being and staff retention improve.
>
> Fabian de Fabiani

Claire Probert, Headteacher at Lancot Challenger Academy in the UK (see 'Spotlight 2') also mentioned the impact that meaning, and the ability and desire to make a difference, can have on staff well-being. She told me – and I have witnessed this first-hand when visiting the school and working with some of their staff – that staff love their job. Despite the usual stressors, their teamwork skills and enjoyment in their work drive their passion.

Our path provides so many opportunities for passion and happiness.

Claire Probert

Academic achievement

Schools in many countries are still primarily measured on academic outcomes. Academic results in key subjects are, for example, regularly compared between countries (Noble 2017; OECD n.d.), and although there are some signs of change, such as the introduction of Character Education in the new Ofsted inspection framework in England (Ofsted 2019b), if we aim to influence national and international education policy to include more focus on well-being, we need to speak the language of policy-makers. This means we need to provide evidence that improving well-being impacts positively on the measurable outcomes they value.

Luckily, such evidence already exists (Adler 2016; Tough 2013; World Government Summit 2017). Stirling and Emery (2016) explain that children are better able and ready to learn when they are mentally well, Public Health England (2014) link the promotion of well-being in young people to academic attainment, and Weare (2015) evidences the impact of well-being programmes and interventions in the USA on behaviour and academic achievement alongside improvements in mental health. Durlak *et al.* (2011) link social and emotional learning programmes to academic achievement and engagement in school.

Breakthrough Magnet School South, in Connecticut, USA, is a pre-K to 8th grade (early years to age 13–14) school where the impact of focusing on Positive Education is evident in its academic results. Breakthrough was one of the first Charter Schools[13] in Hartford, Connecticut, before becoming a Magnet School.[14] Magnet Schools are known for 'developing positive citizen children

---

13 www.charterschoolsusa.com/education-model
14 www.magnet.edu/about/what-are-magnet-schools

prepared for future careers and successful community engagement'. They are open to all, though due to high demand, places are often allocated on a lottery basis. Principal Julie Goldstein explained to me that 75 percent of Breakthrough's students are on free and reduced lunches; 75 percent are African-American and Latino, and 25 percent are Caucasian and Asian. Half of the students live in Hartford, one of the poorest cities in the USA, and half come from surrounding towns, which creates a diverse community. The school has been recognized by Teach for America[15] for their climate and culture and by Magnet Schools of America for observing the 'five pillars' of Magnet Schools.

Students achieve excellent academic results. They are one of the highest-performing schools in Hartford. Julie told me she knows their children are flourishing. They care about each of their students, they know them individually and they do everything they can to help them succeed.

> We're doing our part in enabling the kids to become the future we need them to be.
>
> Julie Goldstein

Another example of the impact of Character Education on academic outcomes is Kings Langley School in Hertfordshire, UK. This is an 11–18 co-educational Academy (state-funded), founded on the Christian values of justice, love and respect. According to the Association for Character Education's website:

> Kings Langley School attributes much of its recent academic success to a dedicated and passionate commitment to developing the character of all its students. In 2002 the school was placed in the bottom 3% of maintained schools nationally. Over the following ten years, the school has been utterly transformed and this year is placed in the top 29% in the country (without equivalences) for GCSE results in virtually every category. Gary Lewis, the head teacher who has been in charge since 2003, says that concentrating

---

15 www.teachforamerica.org

on traditional standards, such as uniforms, helped the school come out of a slump but it was only when he started to introduce character education that the school and its students really started to flourish.

Association for Character Education[16]

◾ KEY TAKE-AWAYS

1. Student well-being/mental health, staff well-being/mental health and academic achievement are essential building blocks of Positive Education.

2. There is significant evidence to show the link between well-being and academic attainment.

3. You don't need vast financial resources to implement Positive Education in your school.

4. Positive Education is most effective when it permeates the whole school.

16 www.character-education.org.uk/kings-langley-school

Chapter 2

UNIQUE CULTURAL CONTEXT

The Finnish education system wouldn't work in the UK on its own. You need the Finnish social infrastructure to go with it. We have different conditions to work with.

Adele Bates

Will Positive Education work everywhere?

The short answer is 'yes'. This book aims to show that Positive Education can be implemented with any age group, in any type of school, in any country, though adaptations may be needed. Geelong Grammar School (see 'Spotlight 1') is a prestigious private school in Victoria, Australia. When introducing Positive Education, they had the financial resources to bring in Martin Seligman and his team for a substantial period of time to design a framework unique to them. They have exceptional facilities and their parents are able and willing to help the local community by funding training for other schools in the area. This cannot be replicated in other schools that don't have the same resources. The principles, however, can be and have been transposed into many other schools, by taking their unique circumstances into account. For example, while Regent International School in Dubai is also an affluent private school, when the Geelong Grammar School team went in to train their staff in

Positive Education and the well-being curriculum was introduced, this was adapted to Dubai and the school's culture.

One of the phases of the international UPRIGHT research programme (see 'Spotlight 3') relates to the adaptation of the programme to different cultural contexts.[1] The Icelandic Health Promoting Schools programme (see 'Spotlight 3') is not imposed on schools; they participate voluntarily and each school can choose how to implement the programme's themes.

The UK's Department for Education (NatCen 2017) highlights that some schools exist to provide for specific needs, for example religious schools with priorities centred around their belief systems, or pupil referral units for children facing significant barriers to learning. At the University of Birmingham (UoB) School (UK), Head of School Rebecca Tigue told me that when developing their policies and practices, these were informed by the fact that they have a number of pupils with significant and varying additional needs; in 2018, out of a cohort of 450, they had 30 students with 'education and health care plans' (EHCPs).[2]

Fabian de Fabiani, Director of Education at the Odyssey Trust and Assistant Headteacher at Townley Grammar School (UK), told me about Townley's ethos centred around educating the whole person. They considered how they wanted their students to leave after seven years at the school – what kind of aptitudes they wanted them to have and what kind of people they wanted them to be. They wanted their students to flourish. Resilience and leadership were their initial values, from which their character and well-being provision evolved organically. Fabian read around the subject and felt inspired by Sir Anthony Seldon's work at Wellington College and Brighton College, but these were highly exclusive private schools in England; Townley Grammar School's vision of character and well-being was around social mobility.

---

1 www.uprightproject.eu/the-project
2 In England, an EHCP is a legal document drawn up for children who have particular educational needs or disabilities, detailing that child's needs and the support and educational provision they require, including the type of school where they should receive that support.

If the independent sector has been doing this for the last 20–30 years, why can't the state sector do it?

Fabian de Fabiani

They therefore developed their own Character Education programme and policies, built around everyone having a right to social mobility and to discovering their purpose. When, a few years later, they decided to form a Multi-Academy Trust and take on the former Erith School, which they re-opened as King Henry School in September 2018, they realized that what had worked at a girls' grammar school[3] could not simply be transposed into a co-educational comprehensive school that had been labelled as 'requires improvement'.[4] They reviewed the school's policies, focused on the language of character and introduced change through a collaborative approach. This is an on-going process. Although Townley Grammar School and King Henry School have curricula closely linked to character, each has a curriculum bespoke to its pupil population.

Seligman *et al.* (2019) refer to the need to consider the unique cultural context as 'cultural immersion' (p.62), an essential consideration when they developed the Gross National Happiness curriculum for Bhutan and similar frameworks which they adapted to the different cultures of Mexico and Peru (Seligman *et al.* 2018). Adele Bates explained to me how Finland's social infrastructure supports its education ethos. For example, Finnish children have much independence in getting to and from school and even relatively young children are not required to be in school when they don't have lessons. This is, however, supported by a thriving system of youth/activity clubs and community-based activities taking place in libraries, so there is always something for children to do and somewhere safe for them to go.

---

3   A grammar school in England and Northern Ireland is a type of state-funded secondary school that is academically selective. Pupils need to pass an exam known as the '11+' to be admitted to a grammar school.

4   'Requires improvement' is a rating given to schools by Ofsted, the UK government's inspection body for schools in England, when they have not yet reached a standard considered 'good'. They will usually be re-inspected within 2½ years.

Positive Education at all stages of education

While this book primarily focuses on Positive Education in schools, Positive Education is possible in higher-education institutions, too. Not only is Positive Education possible in a university, but it can work in a unique, vast institution catering to the educational needs of nearly 60,000 students spread across 30 campuses: Tecmilenio[5] in Mexico is the world's first *positive university* and boasts a robust Positive Education framework. In 2017, the University of Buckingham in the UK became Europe's first positive university and, as I will explore in Chapters 3, 7 and 9, Positive Education strategies have been successfully adopted in French higher-education institutions, too.

The UoB's Year 12 and 13 (age 16–18) is very different to the main school as it has no 'nodal' admissions (see Chapter 1) and selects by attainment at GCSE,[6] though it still retains its focus on character, service, flourishing and developing the humanity of their students.

At the other end of the education age range, Jo Owens, Director of Ethical Leadership at Lichfield Cathedral School in the UK, told me that whilst all pupils at the school participate in the Ethical Leadership Programme, the programme has been adapted to fit the context of early years education so that it would be accessible to the youngest children in the school.

◾ KEY TAKE-AWAYS

1. Positive Education can work in just about any cultural context or age setting, but needs to be adapted to specific circumstances; it is not a 'one size fits all'.

2. Having a clearly articulated ethos and vision helps make the Positive Education adaptations relevant to your school.

---

5   www.tecmilenio.mx/en
6   GCSE: General Certificate of Secondary Education – national subject-specific exams taken by 16-year-olds in England, Wales and Northern Ireland.

SPOTLIGHT 1: GEELONG GRAMMAR SCHOOL

The Timbertop Campus is a beautiful place where you can't help but be present, be spiritual, be mindful, be still.

Rhiannon McGee

History of Geelong Grammar School

An entire book (Norrish 2015) has been written about Geelong Grammar School in Victoria, Australia. It is not my intention to replicate that here, but rather to give you a brief overview of this school and its role in the global development of Positive Education. Geelong is featured in numerous academic articles and the school's website provides an informative timeline[1] of events if you would like to delve into more detail.

Geelong Grammar School started life as an Anglican School with 22 boys in 1855 and became a 'public school' (state-funded school) in 1857 before closing its doors in 1860, having incurred vast debts. It re-opened with a new constitution in 1862, and in 1953, Timbertop Campus,[2] famously attended in 1966 by the Prince of Wales, opened for all 'fourth form' boys (aged 14–15; since 1975, children in what's now known as Year 9, aged 13–14, attend the campus).

From its inception, the school was built on the premise that education was about more than academic achievement, with a focus on character-building through service.

Girls first joined Geelong Grammar in 1970 in the sixth form (age 17–18); the school became co-educational in 1972 and is now the largest co-educational boarding and day school in Australia, with over 400 staff members and 1550 students across four campuses (Norrish 2015).

---

1   www.ggs.vic.edu.au/school/our-school/our-history/timeline/Timeline
2   www.ggs.vic.edu.au/School/Campuses/timbertop

The Geelong Positive Education programme was introduced in 2008 after extensive staff training by Martin Seligman, beginning the school's journey towards being the first in the world to adopt a whole school well-being philosophy based on Positive Psychology.

Positive Education at Geelong Grammar School

In his Foreword to *Positive Education* (Norrish 2015), Seligman describes how a telephone call from a Geelong parent asking him to talk to alumni to help the school raise funds for a well-being centre turned into a sabbatical for his entire family, during which two of his children attended Geelong Grammar School as pupils.

Staff training was crucial to the implementation of Positive Education at Geelong Grammar School, which was intended to benefit staff and pupils. All of Geelong's staff (teaching and non-teaching) received intensive nine-day training from Karen Reivich and Martin Seligman as part of a team of 20 trainers from the University of Pennsylvania. It was during this training that the term 'Positive Education' was coined. In the words of Stephen Meek in the Introduction to *Positive Education*, 'the definition of Positive Education is the bringing together of the science of Positive Psychology with best practice teaching, to encourage and support schools and individuals to flourish' (Norrish 2015, p.xxviii).

From the inception of Positive Education at Geelong Grammar School, the intention was to share the ideas and benefits of Positive Psychology with other schools, which became a reality when 360 teachers were able to attend one of two six-day training courses with the University of Pennsylvania team in 2009, thanks to generous donations from Geelong Grammar's parents. The school now also has an Institute of Positive Education,[3] which carries out research into Positive Education with leading universities and delivers training to schools in Australia and worldwide. Training has also been extended to parents and other family members.

In 2011 the team from the University of Pennsylvania began training staff to train other staff, in order to ensure the sustainability

3   www.ggs.vic.edu.au/Institute

of Positive Education at Geelong. The internal sustainability of Positive Education at the school is separate to the outward-looking work of the Institute. Rhiannon McGee is Head of Positive Education and, although she is attached to the Institute, her role is inward-looking, towards Positive Education within Geelong Grammar School. Her role carries responsibilities across all four campuses, which each have a Positive Education co-ordinator and Positive Education teachers. Rhiannon's role includes overseeing the Positive Education curriculum and piloting new curricula, working with co-ordinators on focus days and other events, and working with heads of department/faculty and the Institute's senior leadership team. Rhiannon is responsible for ensuring Geelong remains authentic, continues innovating in Positive Education and remains at the cutting edge of this growing field. One of her focus areas is staff involvement and parent (and grandparent) engagement. Recently, over 200 grandparents attended a Positive Education workshop!

The Geelong Grammar School model of Positive Education, based on Seligman's PERMA model of well-being (Seligman 2012) plus 'positive health', is displayed on the school's website;[4] it has recently been updated to include an outer circular layer to illustrate the need to learn, live, teach and embed Positive Education (Hoare, Bott and Robinson 2017).

---

4   www.ggs.vic.edu.au/Positive-Education2/Model-for-Positive-Education

Chapter 3

GOALS ASSESSMENT

When you feel that what you're doing has a strong purpose and a strong impact on people's lives, that can fuel you. That's like your reservoir of hope.

Fabian de Fabiani

Goals provide direction

Lopes *et al.* (2013) speculate that it may not be straightforward to find common goals for Character Education on a societal level, so schools tend to set their own objectives and, as I outlined in Chapter 2, each school needs to set its initiatives according to its specific culture. The Jubilee Centre for Character and Virtues (2017) suggests that schools express their Character Education commitment by articulating it within their mission statement. Furthermore, Payne (2018) stresses the importance of common goals in achieving a positive school climate steeped in a sense of community.

Seligman *et al.* (2019) highlight the need to have a robust 'needs and goals assessment' (p.61), yet goals relating to children's citizenship education are, according to Thomson (2010) and Westheimer and Kahne (2004) often imprecise. Speaking to educators, I have found that in practice, many goals relating to Positive Education are vague, as they tend to be aspirational; from a culture-change and stakeholder engagement perspective, however, this can be powerful.

When Geelong Grammar School in Australia embarked on its Positive Education exploration, this was initially a step taken based on an ambitious vision of improving pupil and staff well-being. Similarly, when I interviewed Claire Probert, Headteacher at Lancot Challenger Academy in the UK (see 'Spotlight 2'), her face lit up as she spoke with passion of the vision that drove her relentless drive to change the curriculum at her school and make it character-centric. She was determined to prepare children for life in the 21st century by giving them real-life skills and a palpable sense of opportunity. She wanted them to see 'what life could be like' and strive to achieve their best possible lives. Dan Morrow, CEO of the Woodland Academy Trust in the UK, has a deeply moving, powerful vision driven by his pain in seeing a divided, toxic society and increasing levels of poverty, and his belief in the transformative power of education in giving children hope and a better future. He told me that 'we get to decide the kind of society the children we're educating are going to live in.'

In the short-term, these kinds of wide-ranging, long-term aspirational goals are difficult to measure and are steeped in hopes and wishes rather than measurable outcomes. In the next chapter, however, I will give an example of how bold visionary goals can lead to tangible and sizeable outcomes such as significant cost savings.

Bold, aspirational and broad-ranging goals can create impact in a number of unexpected ways. In a post-18 higher-education institution in France, Kti Dossot, Founder of KtiD Vision to Value, led an Appreciative Inquiry (Hammond 2013; Srivastava and Cooperrider 1990) project which had aspirational goals, initially set by the school's General Manager, then collectively tuned and confirmed by the Appreciative Inquiry steering group comprising around 12 people:

> To enable students to attend our school with a desire to learn, to interact and to have a flourishing career; to better understand the students; to listen to what lecturers, students and alumni have to say about their institution and what they wish to see here in future;

to build, together, the future of the institution in a collective, collaborative, participative, contributory and optimistic manner.

Their 'affirmative topic' (mission statement for the Appreciative Inquiry process) was: 'Together, joyfully, we will build the success and flourishing of our students throughout their future professional journey.' The project, which spanned several months, ultimately involved up to 50 volunteers (teachers, students, other staff and alumni). In Chapters 7 and 9, I will highlight some of the outcomes of their Appreciative Inquiry process.

Fabian de Fabiani, Director of Education at the Odyssey Trust and Assistant Headteacher at Townley Grammar School (UK), links Character Education goals to teachers' sense of purpose and hope. Townley Grammar's Character Education journey began with a clear vision of educating the whole person, promoting social mobility and enabling children to flourish. The three-year plan set in motion for King Henry School by Fabian de Fabiani and Desmond Deehan, CEO of the Odyssey Trust, while also aspirational, is more specific and measurable in the short-term: They want to enable children to express their individual sense of purpose and exhibit self-regulation in identifying the correct choice in difficult situations.

The University of Birmingham (UoB) School (UK) and Crowmarsh Gifford Primary School (UK) began with broad aspirational goals but then narrowed down their objectives to more immediately discernible ones. In recognizing that Crowmarsh Gifford would require a change in ethos in order to introduce Positive Education, Headteacher Flora Barton began by establishing a core set of shared values derived from working with staff, pupils and parents. She soon introduced measurable outcomes, however, such as the goal for teachers to leave at least twice a week without any marking to do. UoB School's core purpose from the outset was to build a new school for the benefit of its community, with a mission to create better citizens. Practical and distinct goals included the school being diverse and inclusive by attracting pupils from four diverse 'nodes' across the city.

Lessness Heath Primary School (UK) began its Positive Education journey with a clear goal derived from a challenge presented to Headteacher Katy O'Connor when she took up her post. The immediate priority was to build trust and relationships. Similarly, Paul Bateson is a teacher who began a determined journey into Positive Education with a clear goal, also derived from a specific set of circumstances. He taught in a working-class school in a deprived ex-mining community in northern England, where the student population was 98 percent white British. He had been teaching there for years, ever since he joined as a newly qualified teacher. Although the environment was challenging, the children were lovely and he enjoyed his work, but then the regulatory inspection framework changed, the school was rated badly and morale amongst staff and students dropped. A staff survey Paul carried out as part of his dissertation for an MA in Education showed that pupil behaviour was a big concern. Then something uplifting happened: A member of staff e-mailed her colleagues to tell them about a troubled student who had displayed exceptional kindness that morning; she asked them to praise the student for this behaviour. It struck Paul that kindness is innate and life is made up of lots of little moments of kindness; he wanted to harness this in school. As a drama teacher and school council co-ordinator, he led a project to encourage kindness, which led to phenomenal outcomes, particularly as it was driven by one person, from the bottom up (see Chapters 10 and 12).

Goals support future evaluation

Positive Education goals tend to be either aspirational and somewhat vague, or more specific and tangible. There is a valid rationale for both, but from an evaluation perspective, the latter can be more useful.

According to the Jubilee Centre for Character and Virtues (n.d.-a), when schools carry out a Character Education self-evaluation process, they can assess their results against national framework goals for education. The Jubilee Centre does, however, warn against 'static' self-evaluation, whereby rather than providing a 'continual feedback loop' for improvement, evaluation is simply used to assess whether an objective has been achieved (Jubilee Centre n.d.-b, p.17).

When researching the effectiveness of well-being programmes and interventions, however, it can be useful to adopt a methodology based on clear goals and measurement of outcomes against those initial objectives. In doing so, empirical data can be obtained to help schools choose interventions that are robust and effective. Meiklejohn *et al.* (2012) describe the goals of a number of school-based mindfulness programmes, then evaluate their effectiveness; Stirling and Emery (2016) recommend having clearly defined goals for any well-being and mental health frameworks in schools to make it possible to evaluate them. In the next chapter, I will explore evaluation in more detail.

KEY TAKE-AWAYS

1. Positive Education goals tend to be school-specific.

2. Positive Education goals can be broad and aspirational, or tangible and specific. There is a place for both, but they serve different purposes. Aspirational goals are great for inspiration and uniting a school community, whereas measurable goals are more useful for research purposes and to evaluate the effectiveness of programmes and interventions.

Chapter 4

EVALUATION

Carefully looking through the Positive Education lens, monitoring the interventions and progress, makes me confident to say these things we're doing together are making a positive difference in school culture, in discipline, in student growth.

Rebecca Comizio

There are different reasons for evaluating Positive Education, and consequently different ways to carry out evaluations.

Evaluation for internal purposes

The Jubilee Centre for Character and Virtues (n.d.-b) differentiates between 'self-inspection' and 'self-evaluation' (p.7). It states that, unlike inspection, evaluation is an on-going bottom-up process that improves teaching and learning and saves time. Berkowitz and Bier (2005) take a similar view, highlighting the importance of using evaluation to drive the improvement and further development of Character Education programmes.

Geelong Grammar School in Australia employs Rhiannon McGee as Head of Positive Education, whose responsibilities include on-going evaluation of the school's Positive Education provision to ensure they remain authentic and innovative. The school also tracks students after they leave to gather longitudinal data relating to their well-being. Internal evaluations at Townley Grammar School in the

UK include listening to students' views. Tweaks to their well-being and Character Education provision are student-driven, based on their half-termly reflections.

New Canaan Country School is an independent pre-K to Grade 9 (age 3–15) school in an affluent part of Connecticut, USA. They are a mission-driven school whose policies and practices centre around educating the whole child and ensuring their pupils flourish. Whilst high academic achievement is a key aspect of the school's ethos, respecting childhood and supporting character development are seen as equally important. As part of the school's commitment to ensuring child well-being is at the heart of everything they do, New Canaan Country School employs Rebecca Comizio as a school psychologist. The school's 'mission skills'[1] – teamwork, creativity, ethics, resilience, curiosity, time management – are a set of six skills similar to some of the VIA Character Strengths.[2] These skills are taught through embedded Character Education (see Chapter 10), targeted interventions (see Chapter 11) and a social and emotional curriculum (see Chapter 9). As part of this curriculum, Rebecca gets involved in the classroom for greetings, feelings check-ins, and social and emotional learning conversations, as well as regular pull-out small group meetings – 'Mrs C's Chats' – with small groups of pupils, based on the Collaborative for Academic, Social and Emotional Learning (CASEL)[3] framework, during which they work on areas such as self-awareness, self-management, social awareness, relationship skills and responsible decision-making. The 'Mrs C's Chats' process is now in its second year, so Rebecca is able to collect data to measure its impact on children.

Berlin Brandenburg International School in Germany is a private school educating children of 68 nationalities, aged 3–18, in state-of-the-art facilities spread across four buildings. When Positive Education consultant Elke Paul, with her extensive background in comparative education, Positive Psychology and yoga, approached the school about introducing a Positive Education programme

---

1   www.countryschool.net/about/mission-skills
2   www.viacharacter.org/character-strengths
3   www.casel.org

two years ago, she was immediately offered a contract. The school already had a great counselling team and a principal interested in Positive Education, but the leadership team understood that, to serve their students better, they needed to place more focus on well-being. Elke explained from the start that her programme would require school-wide culture change and represented a long-term commitment. She began by providing extensive training to staff, resulting in creating a common language of character strengths within the school. Over time, she started to introduce student Positive Education classes as well. Teachers and grade 9–11 students (aged 14–17) take the 'Flourishing at School'[4] well-being survey, which produces a 'Flourishing Profile' for each participant, allowing the school to compare different data points and measure the impact of its programmes.

Lessness Heath Primary School in the UK also regularly measures children's well-being, which gives the staff insight into how well their Positive Education provision is working. Staff regularly complete surveys and Headteacher Katy O'Connor told me it's heartening to see that staff feel they have the time to plan the best possible lessons and that what they do is relevant and makes a difference. When Katy joined the school, introducing whole school Positive Education was a brave decision; she faced pressure to focus on measurable outcomes, so focusing on relationships and behaviour was risky, but she told me she is delighted that the risk has paid off and outcomes have improved each year.

Waters *et al.* (2015) emphasize the need to measure the well-being of students and staff and empirically measure the success of interventions. Flora Barton, Headteacher of Crowmarsh Gifford Primary School in the UK, was also brave in introducing Positive Education and changing the entire culture of her school. An external consultant has run staff stress and well-being surveys for the past three years; each year the results have been outstanding and consistently improving.

---

4   www.flourishingatschool.com

This kind of impact on staff can cause sizeable positive ripples. At a time when, at least in England, many schools struggle for adequate funding, school leaders often resist introducing well-being measures as they worry about incurring costs without tangible returns. As Dan Morrow, CEO of the Woodland Academy Trust in the UK highlighted to me, quite the opposite is possible. Dan introduced Positive Education and has seen a phenomenal unexpected outcome: When he joined the Trust two years ago, they had been losing around 40 percent of their staff per year for a number of years (25–40% staff attrition is currently standard in UK education). Last year, this dropped to 4 percent!

As a business leader, I saved over £100,000 in recruitment last year.

Dan Morrow

LeAF self-evaluation framework

In my LeAF model (see Figure 1.1 in the Introduction), evaluation is represented by the trunk of the tree. LeAF embraces the self-evaluation philosophy described by the Jubilee Centre (n.d.-b) and Berkowitz and Bier (2005). It is a non-prescriptive, holistic, strengths-based framework intended to support an on-going process of improvement. I encourage schools to undergo a four-step process inspired by Appreciative Inquiry[5] and the 'assets, levers, problems' process proposed by Stirling and Emery (2016). For each step, consider who is best placed to carry it out. For example, do you want to issue staff, parent or student questionnaires, or assemble a focus group? If so, from which stakeholder group(s), and what role will the leadership team take? You may even wish to run a full Appreciative Inquiry summit. The possibilities are limited only by your imagination.

---

5   http://appreciativeinquiry.champlain.edu/learn/appreciative-inquiry-introduction/5-d-cycle-appreciative-inquiry

The four steps: 'TWIG'

TREE

Choose which Positive Education element (leaf on the tree) you want to evaluate.

For example, you may decide to look at 'training'.

WHAT?

What is the school already doing?

Here you look at the broad brush-strokes of what is already happening in the element you are looking at that could fall under Positive Education. For example, if you were looking at the 'training' element, you may list things like twilight training sessions on pupil and staff well-being, externally delivered training days on mental health and anything else you are already doing.

INVESTIGATE

How well is the school already addressing that element of Positive Education? What strengths are being used? What strengths are under-utilized and could improve the provision?

If we stay with 'training' as an example, you could delve deeper into what training is being delivered and by whom. Are there, for example, staff members with expertise in well-being whose strengths are being used to full effect, or under-utilized? In Chapter 8, I mention how Lancot Challenger Academy in the UK uses the expertise of one of their staff in this way. Are there members of staff in your school who are particularly strong at delivering training or mentoring and coaching and could be trained in aspects of well-being to aid dissemination amongst the rest of the team?

GALVANIZE!

Schools decide on the actions required to implement further developments. Plans, strategies, budgets and timescales are drawn up in order to facilitate the implementation stage.

For example, you may decide to enrol a member of staff on a Positive Psychology course so they can train other staff within your school. You will need to find out what courses are available, what the timetabling, cover and cost implications are, when and how the training will be rolled out to the rest of the team, and so on.

After TWIG, you need to take action
IMPLEMENTATION

Any actions decided upon during the TWIG process now need to be implemented.

So, with the example I used above, you would now enrol the member of staff on the course and make arrangements for cover while they are away, plus organize training sessions for that training to be disseminated to the wider team.

REVIEW

The LeAF self-evaluation framework is circular. Once a set of actions have been implemented, they will need to be reviewed. Any data gathered can then be evaluated and compared to measure and assess impact.

REPEAT

The TWIG process can be repeated periodically, and of course it needs to be run for other elements of Positive Education (other leaves on the tree – see Figure 1.1).

Evaluation for external purposes
Research and influence

Another reason for evaluating Positive Education is broader and aimed at building a base of empirical evidence to contribute to research in the field and/or influence policy. With a growing number of Positive Education programmes available to schools, Noble (2017) underlines that Positive Psychology principles cannot simply be transferred into education; results seen with adults or on a small scale with children in clinical settings may not automatically be replicated in an educational context. Although there are a growing number of empirically based interventions shown to work in a school environment (Arthur *et al.* 2015; Elfrink *et al.* 2017;

Humphrey, Lendrum and Wigelsworth 2010; Lopes *et al.* 2013; Shoshani, Steinmetz and Kanat-Maymon 2016; Weare 2015; World Government Summit 2017), we need to grow the evidence base. As stated in the World Government Summit (2017) report, if our aim is to change education, we need to 'show that the arguments for Positive Education are true in practice, policy and research' (p.7).

Dóra Guðrún Guðmundsdóttir (see 'Spotlight 3') told me that the Icelandic Directorate of Health gather data on health and well-being indicators for all children, but that programme evaluations take time. There are many well-being programmes across the country's schools – for example, ones on mindfulness and mental health, for which data have just been collected and results will be available by the time this book is published. One of the objectives of the UPRIGHT international research project Iceland is participating in is to 'provide scientific evidence on specific resilience factors which contribute to promote positive mental well-being'. Dóra's team is responsible for leading the 'dissemination, outreach and policy recommendations' element.[6]

At school level, Geelong Grammar School has a strong commitment to contributing to Positive Education research. It has staff in the Institute of Positive Education dedicated to this and has partnered up with the University of Melbourne and Melbourne's Deakin University to carry out well-being research. This year, Sunmarke School in Dubai is one of only four schools worldwide participating in an action research programme with Geelong Grammar School. Action research can be a powerful tool for gathering evidence from school-based practice. This academic year, I have had the pleasure, along with my *Character Toolkit for Teachers* (Roberts and Wright 2018) co-author Elizabeth Wright, of working with two groups of dedicated teachers carrying out Character Education action research. We have supported 'character champions' in the Challenger Multi-Academy Trust[7] with projects

---

6   www.uprightproject.eu/the-project/1935-2/work-package-6
7   www.challengermultiacademytrust.org

ranging from the impact of Character Education on primary school children's confidence in mathematics, to whether singing every day improves children's well-being. We have also delivered training to 'evidence champions' running projects at the Hull Collaborative Academy Trust.[8]

In Germany, the Berlin Brandenburg International School has brought in an external consultant to evaluate the impact of Elke Paul's workshops, serving the dual purpose of providing an evidence base for sharing best practice externally and generating reliable feedback to inform on-going practice within the school.

In the UK, Lichfield Cathedral School and the University of Birmingham (UoB) School have participated in phase one of a short-term impact study run by the Jubilee Centre for Character and Virtues showing the impact of Character Education on children's ability to make moral decisions. The UoB school is also participating in Jubilee Centre longitudinal studies.

Kings Langley School in the UK also works in close partnership with the Jubilee Centre in what Executive Headteacher Gary Lewis calls a 'heady combination' of practical application of Character Education at the school and research and analysis by the Jubilee Centre. Replicability is often used to establish the validity of research, and this holds true in the case of practical application across different contexts. Gary replicated his work at Kings Langley School when he was asked to assist another local school, Cavendish School, which had been rated as 'inadequate' by Ofsted. He adopted an unrelenting approach to introducing Character Education – giving them no choice but to accept the character programme – and did in 17 months what he'd taken 17 years to do at Kings Langley. This challenge had a huge impact, and as Gary told me, was a perfect example of how Character Education can transform a school.

---

8   www.hcat.uk

Inspections and accreditations

Positive Education initiatives can be evaluated for the purpose of
obtaining external accreditations/awards or as part of regulatory
inspection processes. In 2015 the UK's Education Secretary, Nicky
Morgan, introduced the Character Awards,[9] which ran for two years
and aimed to recognize and fund Character Education initiatives
in schools already demonstrating excellence in this area. Townley
Grammar School was 'highly commended' in the 2016 Character
Awards. One of the six questions schools needed to answer in
order to be considered for this award related to evidencing the
programme's impact on children's character.

Gary Lewis, in addition to his role at Kings Langley School, is
Chair of the Association for Character Education (ACE).[10] He and
Tom Harrison (ACE Secretary, Senior Lecturer and Programme
Director for the MA in Character Education and Director of
Education at the Jubilee Centre), carry out thorough school visits
to award schools with the ACE kitemark awarded to 'schools and
colleges that can demonstrate that they take an explicit, planned and
reflective approach to the cultivation of positive character qualities
in their pupils in the interest of human flourishing'.

Regulatory inspections can provide external validation of
the impact of Positive Education. In their last Ofsted inspection,
Lessness Heath Primary School was rated 'outstanding' for the
social and emotional welfare of their children. Sunmarke School was
the first school in Dubai to be inspected within its first year; they
received a 'good' rating. Usually schools have three years before their
first inspection, but Sunmarke requested it early as they wanted
their dedication to both academic achievement and character
development to be recognized. Additional external validation that
what they are doing is working comes from their formal exam
results; they do not select students on ability, yet their results place
them in the top ten schools in Dubai, providing practice-based

9   www.gov.uk/government/news/dfe-character-awards-application-window-now-open
10   www.character-education.org.uk

evidence to support existing research findings (Adler 2016; Tough 2013; World Government Summit 2017) that academic results are strengthened by Positive Education.

External validation of the effectiveness of Positive Education can be more subtle, however. Referrals to child and adolescent mental health services (CAMHS) in the UK are notoriously slow to be processed. Lessness Heath Primary School is able to provide help to children while they are waiting for CAMHS support so they can begin healing. Because of the groundwork the school puts in, their relationship with CAMHS is excellent and nearly all their referrals are accepted.

KEY TAKE-AWAYS

1. Evaluation can be for internal or external purposes.

2. External purposes can include contributing to the research evidence base, influencing policy-makers, satisfying regulatory inspections or supporting award nominations.

3. Evaluations can be scientifically rigorous for research purposes, or more informal.

4. Action research carried out by teachers can be a powerful way to contribute to the Positive Education field of knowledge.

Chapter 5

LEADERSHIP

Get out of your teachers' way!

Julie Goldstein

School leadership is underlined by Public Health England (2014) as an important contributor to children's well-being and their readiness to learn. Morgan (2017) also highlights that school leaders need to prioritize character development, as this influences every aspect of school life. There is extensive literature underscoring the crucial need for school leadership teams to embrace Positive Education (Arthur *et al.* 2015; Berkowitz and Bier 2005; Department for Children, Schools and Families 2008; Roffey 2012; Seligman *et al.* 2019). The Education Support Partnership (2018) stresses that school leaders need to make themselves accessible to their staff; and according to the Jubilee Centre for Character and Virtues (n.d.-a), leaders need to be character role models who actively support their staff in developing their own character strengths.

Positive Education-focused leadership

Julie Goldstein, Principal at the Breakthrough Magnet School South in the USA, is committed to Character Education and has integrated it into the recruitment interview process to ensure all staff are equally committed to the school's values and dedication to Character Education.

Claire Probert, Headteacher at Lancot Challenger Academy in the UK (see 'Spotlight 2') is also dedicated to Character Education. From a behaviour management perspective, she sees this as essential. She has introduced a reward-based system to get children used to character strengths. Whilst she recognizes that this is an extrinsic motivator, she sees it as an opportunity for children to learn about character strengths while the language of character and the behaviours associated with certain attributes become second nature. She runs character-based assemblies and uses the language in everyday situations, such as when giving praise (e.g. 'Thank you for showing respect'). Claire told me her passion comes from wanting to enjoy her time with the children and wanting them to enjoy learning. She sees her purpose as enabling everyone to find their own pathway in life and feels that Character Education allows children to do this.

Rebecca Tigue, Head of School at the University of Birmingham (UoB) School in the UK says it's paramount to have someone on the leadership team who 'champions character', especially as the results may not always be immediately apparent. She said that leaders need to be brave, take a long-term view and believe that they are setting children up to make the right choices in the future. Gary Lewis, Headteacher at Kings Langley School in the UK says that to achieve whole school Character Education requires single-mindedness.

It comes from the headteacher. If the headteacher doesn't believe in it, doesn't believe it's the most important thing, it won't work.

Gary Lewis

Kelly Hannaghan, Well-being Leader at Lessness Heath Primary School, also in the UK, told me that senior leaders are key to achieving whole school Positive Education. She said you need to have a headteacher who really believes in the process and is willing to change the whole culture. Elke Paul told me that whole school Positive Education requires uncomfortable structural changes in addition to culture change. It may be necessary to change the timetable, or to look at the remuneration and recognition of staff as they take on new roles, and consider the repercussions on workload. She says it can be daunting and requires a long-term commitment, and that 'you need to have a driving force' which, in her view, is not necessarily the school's principal, as they already have a job – as a principal.

Dan Morrow, CEO of the Woodland Academy Trust in the UK takes a broad view of leadership: 'Educational leadership should be leading the policy, leading the principles of education, not just leading the practice.' He sees his job title of CEO as 'Chief Environmental Officer' as 'the environment needs to be right for seeds to flourish'. Dan feels that staff morale, well-being and performance are a reflection on the school's leadership. He wants staff and pupils to have a sense of pride and belonging in the school, and told me that to achieve sustainable change and foster creativity, opportunities for failure need to be built in at every level, but that not every leader sees it that way:

> School leaders want to run around and sweep up all the leaves, because they're everywhere; it looks messy. It makes it difficult to appreciate the tree. So all they do is take care of the mess. But is the tree strengthened at all from clearing all of those leaves? No.
>
> The roots are not nourished, so that tree is not going to flourish any more in the future as a result of clearing away all of those leaves; it's cosmetic and it's not long-term. But if, instead, we look at those leaves as part of the natural cycle and still have the resolute focus and authenticity to nurture the roots, in a couple of years' time that tree will be stronger, bigger and bolder than it's ever been.
>
> Dan Morrow

Accessible leaders

Having healthy conversations is a foundational aspect of positive leadership. Patrick Ottley-O'Connor uses the principles of Lencioni's work on cohesive teams.[1] He told me about one aspect that is often

---

1   www.fivebehaviors.com

overlooked: encouraging conflict – having healthy and sometimes difficult conversations. Many people shy away from these, but Patrick encourages an open culture in which people (school leaders or staff) have the courage to initiate the conversations. The basis is trust, which Patrick describes as fundamental to creating culture change and positive schools. When having these open conversations in an atmosphere of trust, the roots of problems are uncovered. Patrick doesn't shy away from emotions.

You don't start a difficult conversation without a box of tissues.

Patrick Ottley-O'Connor

Patrick is also an avid advocate of instilling a culture of coaching, which is something that Katrina Mankani, Director of Positive Education at Fortes Education in Dubai, also supports.

Jo Owens, Director of Ethical Leadership at Lichfield Cathedral School in the UK, told me she has modelled her own leadership style on how she likes to be managed; the leaders she wanted to work the hardest for were those that trusted and appreciated her. She wants to be kind and nurturing and inspire people to give their best.

Role modelling

You can't fake it.

Claire Probert

Claire told me that you have to model the change you want to see and the character strengths you want children and your staff to display. Julie Goldstein is a firm believer in teachers being role models of character rather than relying purely on instruction, as she feels that Character Education is 'much better caught than taught'. Jo Owens told me that students see and watch everything and model their behaviour on what they see.

We are the gatekeepers of the culture of the school.

Jo Owens

Patrick Ottley-O'Connor sees himself as a 'super model' for mental health and well-being – how we treat ourselves and how we treat each other. He quoted the advice of his own (retired) primary school teacher who, when Patrick went to see him when he got his first headship, expecting him to 'stroke his ego' and say 'well done', said: 'It's not about you, lad. A good leader is not a hero, he's a hero maker.' Patrick creates a culture of mental health and well-being by modelling the behaviour, finding the people that 'get it', whatever their role in the school, and nurturing those early followers who will then bring other people on board and 'create a movement'.

Ian Flintoff, Director of Affirm Consulting and former head-teacher, delivers Continuing Professional Development (CPD) and Initial Teacher Training (ITT) in the UK, much of it through Suffolk and Norfolk School Centred Initial Teacher Training.[2] As part of his MSc in Applied Positive Psychology, he undertook a qualitative research study on resilience with four trainee teachers. One finding was that schools can either nurture resilience or undermine it, and that much hinges on how leaders lead – whether they model self-care, for example.

> The leaders that are more self-aware make much better leaders because they know how to look after themselves; they turn up looking fresh on a Monday morning, not exhausted from having worked all weekend. They are more likely to model the self-care that other staff need.
>
> Ian Flintoff

Role modelling can also be a great way to achieve Positive Education goals without needing to spend a fortune. Townley Grammar School is just outside Greater London and therefore does not receive the enhanced funding of a London inner-city school, yet it has successfully brought in a vast amount of Positive Education initiatives. Fabian de Fabiani told me that, first of all, leaders need to make choices about what to spend the money on, but the biggest impact comes from having a clear vision from the top and then embedding this at all

---

2   www.suffolkandnorfolkscitt.co.uk

levels with staff and students. At Townley Grammar, there are staff well-being champions, for example. Then, with training, creativity, free resources available from charities (e.g. 'Time to Change'[3]) and other organizations such as the Jubilee Centre for Character and Virtues,[4] the ripples can spread throughout the school. Fabian told me that Desmond Deehan, CEO of the Odyssey Trust, has a strong sense of purpose and clear vision about what he wants to achieve. Having implemented so much Character Education at Townley, he communicated his vision clearly at King Henry School so staff understood what the school stands for.

In Chapter 1, I outlined some of Dan Morrow's passion for Positive Education and his vision for education as a whole. This stems from his own background, which I feel is a powerful case study in character role modelling:

Dan grew up in what is classed as a highly disadvantaged background, with a single mum who did not earn much working as a cleaner. He was the first in his family to go into higher education and secured a place at Oxford University. His mum and grandmother were the most important people in his life so, when he told his mum he wanted to be a teacher and she told him not to 'waste his life' on teaching, he decided to go for a career that would earn him lots of money. He worked for one of the big global accountancy firms, then ended up living in London and Los Angeles, working in the film industry on big productions such as *Kinky Boots* and *The Hitchhiker's Guide to the Galaxy*. Having lived the high life for a while, he bought his mum a house and did a teacher conversion course so he could pursue his passion. His upbringing has always stayed with him, as has something his granddad said to him: 'Wherever you go, you're going to climb that ladder and you have one job – to hold that ladder for others to follow.'

This is how Dan leads, and this is how he models character.

3   www.time-to-change.org.uk/resources
4   www.jubileecentre.ac.uk/1610/character-education/teacher-resources

Anyone can be a leader

A leader does not have to be someone in an official leadership role. Elke Paul told me that her clients often ask her: 'What if the school's leadership isn't on board?' She tells them that you have to start somewhere, even if you're just one person with a mission. She tells them: 'If this matters to you, it's your duty to do it.' She reminded me of the famous quote:

> Never doubt that a small group of thoughtful, committed citizens can change the world: Indeed, it is the only thing that ever has. (Quote of uncertain origin, mostly attributed to Margaret Mead)

Paul Bateson is an example of committed leadership from someone not in a leadership position. When he decided to launch a kindness initiative in his school, the ripples spread far and wide (see Chapters 10 and 12). He fired up the imaginations of his students, who took ownership of the initiative, and brought most of the staff on board. He did this despite a leadership team who, whilst 'putting up no resistance', did not facilitate what he was doing or make any moves towards adopting a whole school approach. He described his kindness initiative as a 'one man mission'. He achieved outstanding results because of his leadership: He provided tangible examples for others to follow, he made the tasks easy to do, he started small and asked (nicely) for a lot of favours. He was determined and hopeful, made sure he had fun in the process, and used his ability to foster great relationships to cajole and persuade; and he smiled a lot!

Leadership can also come from the students. At Lichfield Cathedral School, student leadership is seen throughout the school. As Jo Owens told me, there are the more obvious roles such as head boy/head girl/prefects, librarian posts, and the junior school's system called 'red caps': Year 4 pupils (age 9–10) wear red caps and, during breaks, it is their job to look out for children who don't have anyone to play with and engage them in a game. Beyond this, though, the school keenly recognizes 'leadership from the back', as there are only a finite number of obvious leadership positions. Jo gave me the example of one 16-year-old boy who is 'not an obvious stand at the front and make a lot of noise' leader, but recognizes he is able to empower and encourage other people to be the best they can be.

It's all about role models; it's not just the ones at the front, it's the quiet ones at the back who look after each other and do the right thing by each other.

Jo Owens

▩ KEY TAKE-AWAYS

1. Whole school Positive Education requires committed and determined leadership.

2. Positive leaders are accessible to their staff, embrace difficult conversations and instil a culture of coaching.

3. Well-being and character need to be modelled.

4. Anyone can be a leader, not just the leadership team. Instead of waiting for the ideal conditions, it is important to start somewhere.

SPOTLIGHT 2: LANCOT CHALLENGER ACADEMY

Curriculum is at the heart of everything. Through curriculum, you can develop the school into what you want it to be.

Claire Probert

Background

Lancot Challenger Academy is a state-funded primary school in Bedfordshire, UK. It is one of eight schools in the Challenger Multi-Academy Trust (CMAT). Its mission, 'embrace challenge, expect excellence', underpins everything. Lancot incorporates *Orchard*, an eight-pupil unit providing for children who have an EHCP[5] for their social, emotional and mental health needs and have been or were at the point of exclusion at their previous setting. Children at Orchard come from all over Bedfordshire; in the long-term, the plan is for them to integrate into the main school.

Headteacher Claire Probert joined the school in 2014 when an Ofsted inspection had rated it as 'inadequate'. The school became part of CMAT in 2015 and Claire became acting Headteacher within two months. She provided direction in line with CMAT's focus on Character Education and providing real-life opportunities for children, not just academic success. Claire designed her own curriculum to drive pupil, parent and community engagement and Character Education; she launched her 'WOW' curriculum – named after the children's reactions to it – with one WOW per term for the whole school. Individual foundation subjects are not taught at Lancot; instead, they are delivered through the WOWs in a cross-curricular, creative approach

---

5   In England, an EHCP is a legal document drawn up for children who have particular educational needs or disabilities, detailing that child's needs and the support and educational provision they require, including the type of school where they should receive that support.

that enables pupils to learn about the world around them. The WOW curriculum has been recognized by Challenge Partners[6] as an 'Area of Excellence'.

Positive Education at Lancot Challenger Academy

The CMAT has a set of four key values: success, working together, aspiration and nurture. Each key value is underpinned by a number of attributes, which vary slightly for each school. Lancot Challenger Academy has a total of 44 attributes that are embedded in the WOW curriculum as well as explicitly taught. Each WOW runs for a term. Examples of past WOWs are:

'Love Lancot'

This enabled pupils and staff to set the school ethos themselves. Each year group produced a promotional DVD and these were presented to the wider community (550+ attendees) at a red carpet 'movie premiere' event in a local theatre.

'Chance for Change'

Every year group created a charity with its own mission statement. They then presented their charities to a panel of judges that selected projects for real-life funding (e.g. charities providing toilets to parts of Africa that don't have any, and earthquake relief support in Nepal). These projects with real impact were actively driven by all children. Claire told me that the children's confidence, knowledge, passion, engagement, ownership and pride were strongly evident in their presentations. 'They're on fire!'

---

6   www.challengepartners.org

'Lancot 3000'

This **WOW** looked at what life would be like in the year 3000. The children turned the school into a living museum, with every year group creating its own exhibitions. They produced QR codes with videos and other information about their displays for parents/visitors to access.

'Lancot Library'

Every child wrote a book, and all books were printed as well as made available on a digital library. The local library has a copy of each book – each child is now a published author!

'The Greatest Showman'

This **WOW** was all about inclusion and diversity and featured a surprise staff dance.

Claire loves the pride and excitement of the WOWs. Everything is about people and relationships; the teachers, children and parents are a team. She describes WOW days as electric. 'There's magic in the air' that children and staff can feel. Each WOW enables staff and children to develop character strengths such as pride, motivation, confidence, collaborative working and overcoming personal challenges. She told me that seeing what it looks like on paper, then in the classroom and finally in the WOW days stays with you. Claire loves watching the parents' reactions, and she wants the experience to stay with the children forever.

> Sometimes you have to stop and look around on these days. It's not just a feeling of 'I did this', but 'we've all done this together'. It's very moving and emotional. You feel awe!
>
> Claire Probert

In order to make these dramatic changes to curriculum delivery and to the culture of the school, Claire had to be brave, resilient and determined. It was a steep learning curve for staff and resulted in dramatic staff changes over a period of three years. All staff are now fully committed to the WOW curriculum and overall Character Education provision in the school, and new staff joining are made fully aware and asked if this is where they see themselves working. Claire has a clear vision that is shared by the senior leadership team and supported by the Trust. It took two to three WOWs for the parents to 'get it', but now it's all they know – particularly those whose children joined the school once the WOW curriculum was already in place.

Alongside the WOWs, financial education is a key component of Character Education at Lancot Challenger Academy. Every class (even the youngest children) has its own bank account, managed by the children. They fund their WOWs by making products and selling them at the WOW events. They have to make a profit to fund the next WOW, but can choose how to spend any surplus. Some classes spend it on termly celebration activities while others save their surplus for a big celebration at the end of Year 6 (age 11, when they'll leave the school). This teaches them about responsibilities, choices and collaborative working.

I have had the privilege and pleasure of spending time at Lancot, delivering staff training, working with children across the age range, and supporting the 'character champions' in their action research projects (see Chapter 4). The impact of Positive Education at the school is palpable and visible everywhere and Claire is an inspirational leader.

Chapter 6

ETHOS AND POLICIES

We catch each other before we fall.

Jo Owens

The need to include Positive Education in a school's overall ethos and policies is prevalent in much of the literature. Seligman and Csikszentmihalyi (2000) state that schools need to be supported in developing climates that enhance strengths. Payne (2018) writes about the impact of school climate on school crime and violence incidents, student engagement and academic attainment, and staff morale, absence rates and turnover. White (2016) highlights that schools need to be pro-active in fostering a positive learning climate by instilling a culture of well-being. The overall school environment is also highlighted by Public Health England (2014) as an influencing factor on children's well-being and their readiness to learn. Their report mentions the importance of school policies, an aspect also underscored by Arthur *et al.* (2015), who set out a framework to assist schools (Jubilee Centre for Character and Virtues 2017).

Culture/ethos

I can't describe it – it's a feeling you have when you walk around the school.

Kelly Hannaghan

From the recruitment interview process through to everyday school life, Breakthrough Magnet School South in the USA has a clear Positive Education focus. The commitment from all staff to being a welcoming and friendly school is supported by systems and structures. When things go wrong, staff and children are used to restorative conversations. For example, there was a girl in middle school who had been making unhealthy choices around substance use and social media and, as a result, she became socially isolated when her friends drew away. The school provided the supportive environment and staff advocates for her and her friends to have a restorative conversation built on openness, honesty, authenticity and trust, and the relationship was consequently repaired. Restorative conversations also take place between adults at Breakthrough Magnet School South.

As I described in 'Spotlight 2', the transformation seen at Lancot Challenger Academy in the UK happened because Headteacher Claire Probert courageously and relentlessly led a programme of culture change throughout the school. Elke Paul told me that when she first started working with the Berlin Brandenburg International School in Germany, she explained to the leadership team that they would need to commit to long-term culture change, with everyone being trained in, understanding and embracing Positive Education, 'from the gardener to the principal'. Patrick Ottley-O'Connor talked to me about the positive impact of creating a culture of well-being in school. You will find some examples in Chapter 12.

Rhiannon McGee, Head of Positive Education at Geelong Grammar School in Australia, illustrated the impact of getting the culture right by telling me about the first time she visited the school's Timbertop campus. She said that from the moment she arrived, she could feel the energy, openness and spirit of the staff there. Every day, they started their morning briefing by sharing 'what went well' – a gratitude exercise. For the students, the year spent at Timbertop is also the year when well-being is at its highest.

That campus is Positive Education encompassed.

Rhiannon McGee

Ian Flintoff told me that, in his research and his experience as a headteacher, he has found that resilience and well-being are all about culture; there is no 'magic bullet' to make pupils or staff more resilient. He said Positive Education can redress the sense of meaning/purpose for teachers by shifting the focus from outcomes to making a difference, which is 'what teachers get out of bed in the morning for'.

At Townley Grammar School in the UK, pedagogy and curriculum are driven by values. Fabian de Fabiani subscribes to the Jubilee Centre for Character and Virtues' (2017) and Nicky Morgan's (2017) view that character is both taught and caught. Fabian describes the ethos as 'the feel of the school'. He and the leadership team have developed what they call the 'character stress test': When issues arise amongst students, how are they resolved? The school has a student chamber and a house council to facilitate restorative justice. New Canaan Country School in the USA and Lichfield Cathedral School in the UK are also driven by their mission, values and ethos.

Policies

When adopting a whole school Positive Education approach, it is essential to ensure that policies are in place to underpin the ethos. The Woodland Academy Trust in the UK, for example, has a policy of offering three paid well-being days off per year to all staff, which they can take for any reason. CEO Dan Morrow gave me an example of a member of staff who suffered the bereavement of a member of her family she was extremely close to. Under a traditional bereavement policy, they would not have been classed as a 'close' family relative, so the staff member would have had to take a day off unpaid for the funeral. Instead, they were able to go to the funeral without worrying about the financial impact of taking an unpaid day off. The policy is supported in practice by headteachers being required to cover the teaching for the well-being days staff take off, so staff don't feel guilty and do use their three days a year. Dan told me that this kind of policy allows leaders and staff to have a 'different conversation' about the value of the person to the school.

Lessness Heath Primary School in the UK has a clear well-being policy and strategy and displays these on its website, alongside information about the available interventions in school, links to external support and photographs of uplifting events. To ensure the physical environment (see Chapter 7) is optimal for learning, the school also has a learning environment policy for teachers which isn't prescriptive, but states key values that need to be adhered to. In 2018, the school was awarded the Optimus Education and National Children's Bureau 'Wellbeing Award for Schools'. Their dedication to a genuine whole school approach to Positive Education is renowned, and the school runs seminars and training days for teachers and leaders from other schools on a regular basis.

Of course, if well-being becomes integral to everything schools do on a national level, the need for individual schools to have well-being policies may disappear. When Adele Bates asked teachers in Finland about their schools' well-being policies, they looked at her in confusion. The introduction of the new national curriculum in 2014 with its seven key themes running through every subject (see Chapter 10) has meant that there is a fundamental, built-in focus on well-being in all aspects of school life.

Adele told me that one fundamental difference between schools in Finland and, for example, schools in the UK, is that at a structural level schools are run differently, allowing a per-student education budget slightly lower than the UK's (and significantly lower than the USA's)[1] to be spent on different priorities. Based on Adele's experience and teacher interviews, in a secondary school of approximately 1000 pupils, for example, there is a principal who does not teach, a vice-principal who also doesn't teach, and one or two assistant principals with a 50 percent teaching timetable and the rest of their time allocated to specific management responsibilities. Reporting directly into the principal are the teaching and well-being support staff. There is no middle management such as subject leaders and heads of year and no meetings for moderation or data collection. Teaching staff and support staff are seen as equal in the school, holding the same

---

1   nces.ed.gov/programs/coe/indicator_cmd.asp

high level of qualifications (minimum to Master's level). One school is likely to have all of the following: a psychiatrist or psychologist, a social worker, a youth worker, a nurse and a counsellor. Teaching staff include subject teachers and special educational needs and disabilities teachers, who are often paid a little more than subject teachers as they tend to be more qualified in their specialism.

Like Finland, Iceland has a holistic national curriculum with a strong focus on themes related to well-being (see 'Spotlight 3'). The document explaining the national curriculum guides (Ministry of Education, Science and Culture with the Directorate of Health, Iceland n.d.) lists the core elements of the Schools for Health in Europe network, of which Iceland is a member country. These include drawing up a healthy schools policy. The voluntary 'Health Promoting Schools' programme has as its main aim to 'support communities/schools to create supportive environments and conditions that promote healthy behaviour and lifestyle, health and well-being of all inhabitants/students/staff' (Department Determinants of Health and Wellbeing, Directorate of Health in Iceland 2018).

■ KEY TAKE-AWAYS

1. A school's culture, ethos and policies are essential to cultivating a whole school Positive Education philosophy and achieving improved well-being, behaviour and attainment outcomes for pupils, as well as improving other measures such as staff well-being, staff turnover and absenteeism.

2. Achieving whole school Positive Education often requires a commitment to long-term culture change, reflected in policies and practice.

3. Restorative practices can be a powerful way to foster positive relationships in schools and to improve the overall school environment.

4. Well-being policies can be introduced in individual schools or at a national level.

Chapter 7

VISIBILITY AND PHYSICAL ENVIRONMENT

The furniture is no longer bolted to the floor.

Kti Dossot

As we saw in Chapter 6, some elements of whole school Positive Education can be felt or experienced as the school's atmosphere/ culture. Others can be seen, either as part of the school's physical environment (e.g. the building, displays, classroom layout) or through the visibility of certain behaviours and communications within and outside the school (e.g. pupil behaviour, relationships between staff and pupils, the way conflict is handled, feedback and marking, staff meetings, newsletters, website, etc.).

Positive physical environment

Berkowitz and Bier (2005) cite research carried out in California showing that schools with the highest Character Education implementation ratings also scored more highly in standardized tests. They provided a number of potential reasons, including the school providing a 'clean and safe physical environment'. Weare and Markham (2005) describe the whole school Health Promoting Schools approach undertaken by members of the Schools for Health in Europe Network (see 'Spotlight 3'), and refer to the school's physical environment as an important factor to consider.

In the UK, the University of Birmingham (UoB) School's physical environment was designed and built with Character Education in mind. The intent was to provide the best possible facilities to support student transition to university undergraduate level. For example, there are university-style science laboratories, and Years 12 and 13 (age 16–18) have the opportunity to get used to university lecture style teaching. Social mobility is a key driver for the school. Given the school's nature, they have strong links with the University of Birmingham. The Year 12/13 block, for example, is physically within the university's Orchard House Learning Resource Centre.[1] There are subtle ways in which the physical environment supports the school's ethos of social mobility: The food technology room, for example, is designed like a university halls of residence kitchen.

UoB School has few notice boards; all important information is on plasma screens around the building, so it can be easily updated. The plasma screens also display character quotes between school notices, and children can suggest quotes to be added. The art rooms were designed with artists in mind, with floor-to-ceiling windows positioned for the best natural lighting. Every floor in the school has accessible, gender-neutral toilets.

Another school built with Positive Education in mind is Sunmarke School in Dubai. The school is very light with lots of indoor and outdoor spaces for mingling. Staff don't prescribe where children should spend their breaks, as that is when friendships form. There is a 'Zen garden' for relaxation and a dark, carpeted well-being room with fairy lights, cushions and yoga mats. Physical activity is encouraged with state-of-the art sports facilities.

Not all physical environments are designed with Positive Education in mind; however, improvements can always be made. In one higher-education institution that Kti Dossot worked with, all chairs and tables were bolted to the floor for security reasons.

---

1   https://intranet.birmingham.ac.uk/as/libraryservices/library/libraries-and-opening-hours/libraries/olrc.aspx

She insisted that during the Appreciative Inquiry process (see Chapter 3), they should be released to create more fluid workspaces. One of the outcomes of the Appreciative Inquiry process has been that the furniture is no longer fixed to the floor and is being moved all the time to allow for different learning environments and situations.

Regardless of the facilities present in a school, character strengths such as respect, according to the Jubilee Centre for Character and Virtues (n.d.-a), can be demonstrated by the way a school's physical environment is looked after by the school community.

If you like yourself and feel great, you look after your environment.

Kelly Hannaghan

Katy O'Connor, Headteacher at Lessness Heath Primary School in the UK, told me the school is in a 'horrible 1950's building, but it's not about that, it's about how we look after things'. The initial focus was to make it the best it could be for the children. They took out carpets and painted all walls a calming light grey, which also showed the children that the school was a space to be proud of. All classrooms have sensory boxes and well-being boards. When Positive Education was introduced, children were encouraged to be environmental leaders, and the school's big field plays an integral part in this. During a staff training day, a set of six school values were decided together. These core values are at the centre of everything the school does, which includes taking responsibility for the school's physical environment. Staff well-being was also considered when looking at improvements to the physical environment. The staff space has a new kitchen, new carpets, new blinds and a staff well-being board.

You don't have to avoid looking at well-being if you don't have the budget for it.

Kelly Hannaghan

When the Positive Education work began at Lessness Heath Primary School, there was no well-being budget. The well-being budget now essentially covers Well-Being Leader Kelly Hannaghan's salary. She's had to be very creative to find solutions to improve the school's environment, and much of that hinges on individuals taking responsibility. Time is another consideration. The 'change team' meetings take place monthly at lunchtime, but although this encroaches on staff personal time, they find there is benefit to spending time together planning and updating each other on progress. Staff value 'being part of something they, families and children see as important'. They see that what they are doing is 'reshaping children's futures'. It gives them hope when children that have come from traumatic/deprived backgrounds have bold aspirations. For example, one child told Kelly: 'I can't wait to become an inspirational speaker!'

Teachers play a role in creating a positive school environment by using the strengths of *creativity and appreciation of beauty and excellence*.[2] Humphrey, Lendrum and Wigelsworth (2010) describe how in all their school visits, social and emotional aspects of learning (SEAL) was felt in tangible ways with pupil SEAL work being placed on display. However, this was more purposeful in some schools than others, as 'in some, it was clearly a "box ticking" exercise with little consideration of purpose'. Other schools, however, used the displays as visible reminders of what children had learnt over the course of the SEAL programme. The Department for Children, Schools and Families (2008) also describes a 'clean and attractive physical environment, including displays of pupils' work', as one of the factors that create a positive climate in the classroom.

Shankland and Rosset (2017) describe 'Secret Strength Spotting', a beautiful practical activity that provides a visible way to improve a classroom's climate. Pupils are paired up to observe each other and make a note of the other person's strengths for a week, though they don't know who has been assigned to observe them. Pupils then jot down the strengths and brief explanations of how they saw the other pupil use them and post them somewhere visible in the classroom.

---

2   www.viacharacter.org/character-strengths

Children in the Foundation Stage (age 3–5) at Sunmarke School have a 'kindness elf' for strengths spotting. They 'spot' each other doing good things, write notes and put them into the elf's bag. If they can't write yet, they tell the teacher, who then writes it down for them. Each classroom has a wall with faces depicting different moods. Children place their name tag under the face they feel matches their mood as they arrive in school. As the day goes on, if their mood changes, they can move their name to different places. This teaches them emotional intelligence from an early age in a way that is constantly visible and therefore reinforces the learning.

Adele Bates told me about one primary school in Finland that has a punchbag in the corridor that anyone can hit when they feel the need to. In *Character Toolkit for Teachers* (Roberts and Wright 2018), Elizabeth Wright and I describe a range of activities that make Positive Education visible throughout the school.

Jo Owens, Director of Ethical Leadership at Lichfield Cathedral School in the UK, told me that theirs is a community where people 'quietly look after each other'. It can be felt as part of the school's culture, and is reflected in the school's physical environment with little touches such as the staffroom kindness display.

Lancot Challenger Academy's 'WOW' events (see 'Spotlight 2') are a great example of Positive Education seen in the school's physical environment as well as the school's communication with the outside world. Evidence of the WOW events can be found in displays throughout school, and at times the work is taken into the community.

Visible Positive Education

Morgan (2017) writes that character strengths and values need to be visible throughout the school, echoing the Jubilee Centre for Character and Virtues (n.d.-c) who state that, for a school to be deemed a 'school of character', there needs to be visibility of character virtues within and outside of the school (e.g. in school displays and in communications with the outside world). They describe visibility as including clear communication of the school's

Character Education ethos to parents combined with evidence of parental engagement with it. Finally, they say that the school's stated mission should make clear reference to the development of character, and that this needs to be actively encouraged in school.

When Claire Probert took on the headship at Lancot Challenger Academy, she spent over a year on promoting 'positivity' as a keyword. This was something she felt the school needed at the time, and it was visibly manifested throughout the school. Everyone took a 'positivity pledge', with a visible reminder on staff lanyards. The pledge included a commitment to doing the 'little things', such as paying compliments to colleagues and refraining from making hurtful comments. Claire described this as a 'militant focus on positivity'. This included an insistence on discussing any issues as they arose and addressing them, rather than moaning and talking about things behind each other's backs. She insisted that staff were models of positivity.

Kings Langley School in the UK communicates its Character Education vision with clarity through assemblies, letters sent home to parents, poster displays in school and the use of social media. For example, a quick glance at the school's Twitter account as I am writing this chapter shows the students using the character strength of curiosity by tasting unusual fruit and healthy snacks at lunchtime; the latest newsletter includes a message from Headteacher Gary Lewis about the school's focus on character and the aim of ensuring the happiness and well-being of everyone in the school. The school runs weekly/fortnightly character strength themes (e.g. 'kindness fortnight'), during which all teaching and non-teaching staff are required to go out of their way to display that strength. Gary Lewis has adopted a firm approach on ensuring Character Education is visible throughout the school. He sees this as 'doing what is crucial in schools – forming relationships'.

> When you force them to do it and they see the impact, it becomes self-fulfilling.
>
> Gary Lewis

Part of the teacher recruitment programme at Kings Langley School includes ensuring potential staff buy into the Character Education programme.

When Paul Bateson launched his kindness project in his previous school, he asked staff to be on the lookout for acts of kindness; students could then earn badges that would accumulate points towards a reward trip. Before launching the project, Paul wanted to demonstrate kindness as some of the students didn't think of themselves as kind, or thought that it was only possible to be kind if you have money. Having previously discussed it with the school council, he and a number of student volunteers went into school early one morning and 'peppered the school with kindness':

- They left 'Have a Nice Day' post-it notes on people's desks.
- They left 'thank you' notes for the cleaners and caretakers.
- They tidied up people's desks.
- They stuck coins to vending machines.
- They left bags of sweets in the social areas.
- They left messages on mirrors in the toilets (e.g. 'You look beautiful').

Later that morning, during Assembly, Paul asked whether anyone had noticed anything strange in school, and children started commenting on what they'd found; he then explained the project. He told me it made him feel great to see the students' responses to the acts of kindness and to the initiative overall. Chapter 13 will highlight more of the emotions that teachers and school leaders feel when they implement Positive Education initiatives.

Rebecca Tigue made me chuckle with the story of 'kettlegate' to illustrate how Character Education permeates school life at the UoB School. A kettle disappeared from one of the staff work spaces and it became a protracted saga, with kettles moving around and nobody owning up to what had happened to the missing kettle. It became a standing joke, but eventually someone said 'we need to stop this – it's not the behaviour of staff at a school of character!'

During Jo Owens's first year at Lichfield Cathedral School, she was a Year 8 (students age 12–13) form tutor and there was a desire amongst staff to do something special for that year group, as it can be a bit of a 'flat' year. The 'Year 8 Celebration Cup' event was created; everyone would have the opportunity to celebrate and share, during their daily 15-minute form period with their form tutor, a skill or quality that had nothing to do with academic ability. Having been a Year 8 form tutor in other schools, Jo wasn't sure how this was going to unfold. In the first week, the first pupil whose name was on the list had forgotten and not brought anything, but another volunteered to step in. He described his favourite activity outside of school, why he loved it so much, the challenges and learning opportunities it presented him with, how it enabled him to engage with his community, how much he loved helping younger participants in the activity and his hope to move into a formal leadership role as he got older. The rest of the class were mesmerized! They sat and listened in total silence, then asked him lots of questions at the end. This was a boy who was really quiet, 'not an obvious stand at the front leader' (see Chapter 5).

To see how he bloomed under the appreciation was amazing!

Jo Owens

The school's leadership team is keen for prospective parents to get to 'feel the culture' when they visit, so they hold open days rather than open evenings and staff are specifically told not to teach a 'show lesson' on those days. In this way, parents can see Positive Education in action at the school.

At Crowmarsh Gifford Primary School in the UK, Positive Education is visible to the entire school community inside and outside school through the use of its themes and hashtags, such as #BePhenomenal and #HotChocFri. The latter is a regular event where children are selected at random from those consistently role modelling school values to sit down for hot chocolate with the headteacher. A similar initiative is also in place at Lancot Challenger Academy. #BePhenomenal is the big theme at Crowmarsh Gifford, which ties in with their 'Purple Learning' philosophy (see Chapter 1). Parents can fill in sheets to describe things their children have done outside of school. Headteacher Flora Barton told me the story of one boy who had undertaken a difficult physical challenge over the half-term holiday. His parents sent a #BePhenomenal sheet to school to share his achievement, explaining how he'd fallen and slipped numerous times but, despite his struggles, had persevered and eventually succeeded. Another way Positive Education is highly visible at the school is through pupil behaviour, which Flora told me is manifested particularly in excellent manners that external visitors notice when they go to the school. Rather than focusing on the 'pleases and thank yous', the school focuses on promoting awareness of others – being spatially aware (e.g. stepping out of people's way), showing empathy, giving people time, making eye contact, asking people how their day has been.

> When you're well-mannered, you're aware of other people; you're aware of other people's emotions, of their feelings, of what they need, even when they're not saying it.
>
> Flora Barton

The focus is on 'making people feel you care about them'. Flora told me that if you ask the children what you can do to show someone you care, they always say 'smile'. Although the school engages children in many 'random acts of kindness' (see Chapter 12), Flora told me 'they know the biggest act of kindness is giving someone a smile and letting them know you're there and thinking of them.'

Having a therapy dog in school is one way to make Positive Education highly visible. Lessness Heath Primary School introduced Lola in 2018. She lives in the headteacher's office but can often be seen around school. Staff and children love stroking her and some Year 6 (age 10–11) children take her out for walks during the day. Lola even has her own blog!

■ KEY TAKE-AWAYS

1. A school's physical environment can positively impact on the well-being and character development of children and adults in a school, which can, in turn, be evident by how well the school community looks after its environment.

2. Positive Education can be visible in school through behaviours, displays and communications.

SPOTLIGHT 3: NATIONAL AND INTERNATIONAL INITIATIVES

It's not enough to teach something in a lesson. You need to change the culture.

Dóra Guðrún Guðmundsdóttir

I was fortunate to be able to interview Dóra Guðrún Guðmundsdóttir, Head of the Division of Determinants of Health at the Directorate of Health in Iceland – a government agency under the Ministry of Welfare – who told me about the three initiatives described below. These show how national policy and international co-operation can support schools in achieving whole school Positive Education.

Iceland: Health Promoting Schools

Work on *Health Promoting Schools* spans all stages of education in Iceland. It began in 1999, then was reintroduced in 2004 and 2008, but it was the introduction of the *health and well-being pillar* in the 2011 national curriculum guides for all age groups that made it possible to truly drive the initiative forward and adopt a whole school approach to health and well-being. The health and well-being pillar encourages schools to promote a number of physical and mental health attributes, amongst which are a positive self-image, an understanding of feelings, positive communication and mental well-being, ultimately supporting the development of the whole child to allow them to 'thrive in society and cooperate with others' (Ministry of Education, Science and Culture and Directorate of Health, Iceland n.d.).

Dóra told me that the introduction of this pillar to the national curriculum guides marked a fundamental change, as it formally acknowledged that health and well-being were essential components of education. She stressed the importance of a whole school approach involving students, parents and staff. She also highlighted that, although the programme has been running for a number of years, it takes time for change to happen, particularly as teachers were not previously trained in health and well-being, so this now needs to filter through into schools with teacher training. Data are still being gathered and analyzed to evaluate impact, but it is hoped that it will be significant.

The other pillars of the national curriculum guides are literacy, sustainability, democracy and human rights, equality and creativity (Ministry of Education, Science and Culture and Directorate of Health, Iceland n.d.). Much like in Finland, the Icelandic curriculum pillars do not prescribe exact content or methods of delivery; instead, schools and teachers are required to ensure that content, resources, pedagogy, and school policies and procedures reflect the six pillars.

UPRIGHT: An international research project

UPRIGHT, a project funded by a European Union Horizon 2020 research grant, stands for 'universal preventive resilience intervention globally implemented in schools to improve and promote mental health for teenagers'.[3] Launched in 2018 it will run for four years and follows the prevention and promotion model of Positive Education (see Chapter 1). Like the Icelandic Health Promoting Schools programme, UPRIGHT takes a holistic approach involving the adolescents themselves, their families, and education professionals. UPRIGHT runs in Iceland, Poland, Spain, Denmark and Italy. Over the four years, the project is divided into 'work packages'. Dóra Guðrún Guðmundsdóttir will lead work package 6: dissemination, outreach and policy recommendations.

SHE: Schools for Health in Europe

Iceland is also one of 33 countries participating in Schools for Health in Europe (SHE)[4] – a health promotion network founded by the World Health Organization (WHO) in 1991 and running as an independent non-governmental organization co-funded by the European Union and

3   http://uprightproject.eu
4   www.schoolsforhealth.org

the WHO since 2017 – aiming to ensure all schools promote health, where health is defined as mental, social and physical well-being.[5] SHE operates on a set of core values (equity, sustainability, inclusion, empowerment, democracy) and six 'pillars' (whole school approach to promoting health, participation, school quality, evidence, school and community).[6] SHE run a number of 'SHE Academies', courses aimed at researchers and practitioners in education and health. Additionally, international researchers can join SHE's research group to support the project in its on-going research output to provide a solid evidence base for health-promoting interventions.

---

5   www.schoolsforhealth.org/concepts/concept-health
6   www.schoolsforhealth.org/concepts/she-values

Chapter 8

TRAINING

Everything has to begin with the staff.

Flora Barton

Continuing Professional Development

As I outlined in Chapter 1, stress contributes greatly to the loss of teachers from the education system, and to mental health issues for teachers. One of the causes of stress cited by the National Union of Teachers (2013) is a lack of career and further development opportunities. Continuing Professional Development (CPD) is therefore an important factor to be considered for the well-being of teachers, and to ensure teachers are attracted into and retained in the profession. Additionally, staff need training to deliver Character Education (Berkowitz and Bier 2005) and well-being lessons (Waters *et al.* 2015); having a strong grounding in pedagogy does not provide the Positive Psychology knowledge to deliver well-being interventions or teach well-being lessons. Arthur *et al.* (2015) and Morgan (2017) state that school staff should receive training in Character Education.

Katy O'Connor, Headteacher at Lessness Heath Primary School in the UK, loves 'growing people'. Her school has many newly qualified teachers and she hopes that, through the CPD available to them, her school will be able to buck the trend of teachers leaving the profession in droves. She believes that she can do this by providing them with consistency and a different kind of pressure – pressure that contributes to the teachers' sense of purpose.

At Geelong Grammar School in Australia, staff training in well-being and Positive Psychology has been extensive, forming an essential part of the launch of Positive Education at the school. This focus on staff training continues to this day, with all new Geelong staff being trained in Positive Psychology, and the team from the school's Positive Education Institute delivering training to other schools in Australia and internationally. They were invited to Regent International School in Dubai in 2016 to train their teachers in Positive Education. Training all staff, not just teachers, in Positive Psychology ensures consistency throughout the school. The day before I interviewed Katrina Mankani, Director of Positive Education at Dubai's Regent International and Sunmarke Schools, she had trained 70 learning support staff. Katrina loves the impact this training has on the staff's well-being and on the leadership team's relationship with the staff. Elke Paul, Positive Education Consultant at the Berlin Brandenburg International School in Germany, has been to Geelong Grammar School twice to learn from them. She has interviewed many Positive Education practitioners and teachers and has learnt a key lesson:

You start with teachers first.

Elke Paul

In the two years she has been at Berlin Brandenburg International School to date, Elke has spent most of her time on staff education. All staff attended a three-day Positive Psychology workshop to learn the pillars of well-being. The workshops included staff from across the year groups and both teaching and non-teaching staff; as the school is spread out across three buildings, learning opportunities are often lost. Mixing people for the training was deliberate, to improve collaboration and trust. The first thing Elke told staff on the first day was: 'This training is for you. I don't want you to even think about how you can incorporate it into the classroom.' Initially, staff kept asking for classroom ideas, but after a couple of hours they started to relax into the training and understand the need to look after themselves. The training provided a common language at the school. Everyone understood character strengths, for example, so teachers started to talk to each other about character and well-being. Elke has received countless e-mails from staff telling her how they have benefited. One recent e-mail told her: 'I'm changing – thank you!'

As a result of Elke's training, two teachers have started their own Positive Education programme without her input. They introduced a classroom board with the title 'I feel stressed when...' that children contributed content to. They have also begun embedding Positive Education in their subject curriculum. Others want to bring Elke into their classes to teach students directly. Her role in school is now evolving as the school's needs change, but it all had to begin with staff being trained for their own well-being. Elke told me that often teachers will resist at first, seeing Positive Education as 'just another programme' that will require them to have a bigger workload. She worked hard to convince teachers that Positive Education, rather than being a bolt-on, is a bottom-up approach and that it is very much about their well-being. This is, in her opinion, a key message that leaders need to communicate to staff. Of course, there will always be some teachers who are not interested, but Elke puts her focus on nurturing the teachers who are interested in, and motivated to learn about, Positive Psychology. Those early followers are the ones that will shift the culture, as we saw in Chapter 5.

Flora Barton, Headteacher at Crowmarsh Gifford Primary School in the UK, also firmly believes that 'everything has to start with staff'. As well as introducing Purple Learning (see Chapter 1), when she set about changing the culture of the school, she brought in Andy Cope and his 'Art of Brilliance'[1] team to train the staff before the team spent an additional day working with the children.

You guys have to be willing to step out of your comfort zone if we're going to be teaching the kids this!

Flora Barton

---

1   www.artofbrilliance.co.uk

As part of the Health Promoting Schools programme in Iceland, participating schools (and communities) and those wishing to join the programme have the opportunity to attend annual seminars, conferences and workshops. Additionally, staff at participating schools can log into the Directorate of Health's interactive web portal[2] to receive guidance and ideas for implementing the programme into their school.

Kings Langley School (UK) delivers its extensive Character Education programme, thanks to all teachers being trained in character development. Lancot Challenger Academy (UK) makes use of the mental health expertise of the Orchard Provision Leader to develop all school staff. She delivers regular training to the whole school. All teaching and associate staff at Townley Grammar School (UK) have been trained in Seligman's PERMA model of well-being (Seligman 2012) so they can embed this in their teaching and use it in their own lives. They have also received training in mindfulness and, thanks to this, many lessons now start with a period of quiet reflection.

When the Odyssey Trust (UK), which includes Townley Grammar School, re-opened the former Erith School as King Henry School, all staff received well-being/PERMA training, which reinvigorated them and gave them a renewed sense of purpose and engagement. This marked the start of an entire change of culture at the school, which is still in progress. According to Odyssey Trust Director of Character Education and Well-being and Townley Grammar School Assistant Headteacher Fabian de Fabiani, the behaviour policy became 'less top heavy' and more collaborative, focusing on the language of character. Staff at King Henry School have also, like their counterparts at Townley Grammar, been trained in mindfulness.

When the new Ethical Leadership Programme was launched at Lichfield Cathedral School in the UK, all form tutors received training in this. The school's commitment to training staff in character and well-being is on-going; in 2018, my *Character Toolkit for Teachers* (Roberts and Wright 2018) co-author Elizabeth Wright

---

2   www.heilsueflandi.is

and I spent half a day in the school, delivering Positive Education training for teachers from early years (teaching children age 3–5) to Years 12 and 13 (age 16–18). We provided them with some background knowledge on character and well-being, but the focus was mostly on practical implementation in the classroom and whole school.

> After celebrating excellent public exam results, we realized that we needed to ensure our school focus continued to include positive approaches to well-being and mental health, for staff and for students. As a result of the CPD provided by Frederika and Elizabeth, we are re-structuring our PSHE/SMSC[3] programmes to focus more explicitly on character development and positive psychology.
>
> Jo Owens

External training and development providers play a role in the introduction and development of Positive Education in schools. In Norfolk and Suffolk in the UK, schools bring in Ian Flintoff of Affirm Consulting to deliver personal well-being training to staff and headteachers. He trains educators in team and individual strengths and models of resilience, based on the principles of Positive Psychology. Anni Silverdale Poole, Director of HLS for Whole School Well-Being and author of Simply Being YOU, provides coaching to teachers and headteachers. She told me that, for new headteachers particularly, 'their world is spinning like a fairground and they so often become totally lost in the content of their role'.

CPD within the Woodland Academy Trust in the UK is extensive and applies to all staff. Seventeen members of staff are doing a Master's qualification on topics as diverse as reading, metacognition, character development and finance; all are supported in this by the Trust.

The UK's University of Birmingham (UoB) School also has a great commitment to staff CPD. Teachers are guaranteed ten days of INSET[4] per year. Head of School Rebecca Tigue told me that Year 9

---

3   PSHE: Personal, social and health education. SMSC: Spiritual, moral, social and cultural.
4   INSET: In-service training.

(age 13–14) students have been working through the intensive and challenging *Project Wayfinder*[5] – a programme developed in the USA to improve young people's mental health by helping them find purpose and meaning. All staff who deliver the programme at UoB School have to undergo a two-day intensive training programme – which includes keeping their own journals, working through several exercises together and discussing the shape of the programme – as part of their CPD so they can understand the emotions and challenges the students will face. The additional benefit is that it is a well-being intervention that helps staff find their purpose, too. Rebecca told me that working at UoB School changes people – staff do more volunteering than they used to, and some have changed careers. One teacher has become a social worker, and two non-teaching staff have become teachers.

Now I have seen what schools can be like, I want to be a part of it.

Teacher at UoB School

In Finland, teacher CPD is embedded in the culture. Adele Bates told me that teachers are highly trained – all are qualified to at least Master's level in their subject – and see themselves as practitioners and researchers; they take their CPD very seriously. All textbooks in Finnish schools are written by teachers; the system supports them by allowing them to take sabbaticals to write textbooks in their subject. For teachers to progress into leadership roles, they undergo a six-month training programme alongside their teaching responsibilities. They do this by attending evening and weekend lectures, and the schools pay for their training to support their career development.

With all this training comes complete classroom autonomy for Finnish teachers, which, while providing many advantages in terms of curriculum delivery and removing the stress of potentially damaging judgemental observations, can also present disadvantages. Adele gave me two examples: One teacher she observed was incredibly skilful. Adele said watching her was 'like watching a

---

5   www.projectwayfinder.com

ballet'; she kept catching children just before trouble started. When Adele told her what a joy it had been to observe her lesson, and that people must tell her all the time what a great teacher she is, the teacher burst into tears, as nobody had ever observed her and therefore nobody had ever told her this! Another (newly qualified) teacher, on the other hand, was really struggling in her lesson, but because there are no heads of department to provide mentoring and observations, she had nobody to give her any guidance on how to improve her practical teaching skills and reduce her stress levels as a result. As Adele told me, there are advantages to lesson observations, as long as they are done in the spirit of supporting and developing teachers in a positive way. Dan Morrow, CEO of the Woodland Academy Trust, told me that leaders need to stop micro-managing teachers, but that coaching is essential. In the Trust, they now only do peer observations, so staff still get the supportive coaching and mentoring aspect of being observed, without the value judgements they fear may come from their line managers.

Initial Teacher Training

Initial Teacher Training (ITT) should cover more than pedagogy and include training in well-being and educating the whole child (Arthur *et al.* 2015; White 2016). Compulsory guidance on teachers' own mental health and well-being is recommended by the Education Support Partnership (2018).

> There is a crisis of retention in teaching, but I think that actually, Character Education and well-being training for newly qualified teachers or training teachers along these lines can really help with the retention crisis.
>
> Fabian de Fabiani

Despite this, ITT provision of well-being training is still not as widely available as one might hope. I have seen and been told about a few teaching schools in the UK that provide this, but it is not widespread yet. Given how much CPD is required around the world in this area, it would appear that the majority of existing teachers have not been trained in Positive Psychology or Character Education. Dóra Guðrún Guðmundsdóttir told me that, despite the Health Promoting Schools programme having been running for a few years in Iceland, the change required for well-being to become central to schools is slow, because training still needs to catch up; ITT needs to change and include health and well-being.

There is, however, hope for the future as things are beginning to change. In the UK, Ian Flintoff works with Suffolk and Norfolk School Centred Initial Teacher Training, which has a philosophy of 'no trainee will feel alone'; well-being is a big focus of the ITT course and trainees appreciate the support they get. During his qualitative research study of four trainee teachers, Ian looked at their understanding of resilience and what difference it made to their well-being. He found that the best schools were those that became a surrogate home, where trainees felt safe, secure and valued and received great mentoring. These teachers were the most successful. Ian told me that many trainee teachers come from other careers and often have unrealistic expectations of success. He described their first term as a 'firestorm' and said school leaders need to understand that it takes longer than one year for trainees to get a sense of perspective and reach the point where they realize that the job is about making a difference to young people.

> Success is not about them mastering skills, but about making a difference.
>
> Ian Flintoff

Trainees that had a well-developed support network in their training environment and their family and friends did better than those who had a limited support network and consequently felt isolated. Those teachers who took time out were also coping better than those who never stopped working. One trainee, for example, struggled as he had given up his favourite hobby due to lack of time. He told Ian that he felt he had 'lost part of his life'. Once he reintroduced the hobby into his life, he became more resilient to the challenges of his new profession. In his training, Ian uses Johnson *et al.*'s (2014) framework of conditions supporting early career teacher resilience, which includes the importance of school culture, the connectedness felt by and support received by teachers, and trainee and early career teachers' ability to self-reflect.

The UoB School places great importance on self-reflection; it is part of the training for newly qualified teachers in the school. New Canaan Country School in Connecticut, USA has an apprentice teacher in every K–6 class (age 5–12). Not only does this give all children additional classroom support, but it enables trainee teachers to learn on the job while being supported by a qualified and experienced teacher. Many end up staying at the school after their apprenticeship is complete.

■ KEY TAKE-AWAYS

1. CPD is important for the well-being and mental health of teachers.

2. Training teachers in Positive Psychology and Character Education is important for their own well-being and character development, and to ensure they can support and teach children in these areas.

3. Improved CPD can reduce teacher attrition rates.

4. External trainers, coaches and other providers have a role to play in teacher CPD.

5. CPD includes schools supporting staff in obtaining further qualifications.

6. Supportive on-going coaching and mentoring, including lesson observations, can form an important element of CPD.

7. ITT programmes need to include more than pedagogy – teacher well-being and how to teach children, directly and indirectly, about well-being and character needs to be built into ITT curricula.

8. A strong support network, inside and outside of school, a welcoming school culture and opportunities for self-reflection are essential for the resilience of newly qualified teachers and their long-term success as teachers.

Chapter 9

WELL-BEING/ CHARACTER CURRICULUM

Well-being, mindfulness, altruism, character – these need lessons or space in the curriculum itself, not just as part of other curriculum areas. Kindness, for example, needs to be taught, especially as it's not always demonstrated at home or in the world; it needs to be demonstrated, it needs to be practised, it needs to be modelled, it needs to be taught and it needs to be rewarded.

Paul Bateson

Do we need a well-being/character curriculum?

Stirling and Emery (2016), Waters *et al.* (2015) and Weare (2015) present evidence suggesting that an explicit well-being curriculum is worthwhile. Morris (2012) makes the distinction between 'education as happiness' and 'educating for happiness' (p.696). He describes the latter as schools providing 'explicit guidance to their pupils on how happiness might be achieved in life and not just assume that happiness will result from the ordinary activities of school life'. He explains, in detail, how this is done through the happiness curriculum at Wellington College, UK, in his book *Teaching Happiness and Well-Being in Schools* (Morris 2015). Waters (2014) makes a strong case for a well-being curriculum, advocating that schools should teach students Positive Psychology tools to improve well-being while also teaching them to recognize and reduce the symptoms of mental ill-health (e.g. depression).

The Jubilee Centre for Character and Virtues refers to character being both *taught* and *caught* (Jubilee Centre for Character and Virtues 2017, n.d.-a, n.d.-b, n.d.-c, n.d.-d), with specific self-evaluation frameworks for each. In this chapter, I will provide examples of taught character, whereas in Chapter 10, I will explore the way schools can promote character through children *catching* it from role models and the school environment.

Milson (2000) illustrates one case study, backed by evidence of similar practices in other schools in the USA, of a school creating a bespoke character curriculum. Despite some criticisms relating to the specific approach adopted, the overall results show that this can be a useful way to educate children to grow into compassionate and responsible citizens. White and Warfa (2011) describe an action research programme in East Anglia, UK, where a Character Education programme had a positive impact on the school's climate, staff morale and student behaviour, in addition to the school being better able to meet the students' 'social, emotional and cognitive needs'.

Taught Positive Education in practice
Taught Character Education at the University of Birmingham School

In order to accommodate taught and caught Character Education, the University of Birmingham (UoB) School has extended the school day beyond the traditional UK school hours. The school day runs from 8.30am to 4pm and includes 3.5 hours per week of 'Enrichment' sessions in the school timetable (see Chapter 10), plus a week in July where they explore character through challenge and opportunity. In addition, there are 1.5 hours of taught character curriculum delivered, for example, by tutors, in assemblies, and

partly in PSHCE, SRE and CEIAG,[1] plus an hour a week dedicated
to PLAD,[2] where they ensure they meet statutory requirements but
do so through a character focus. This is taught by staff trained in
these areas. Years 12 and 13 (age 16–18) students have two hours of
Enrichment on Thursday afternoons.

Character taught through Enrichment

The Enrichment programme at UoB School is designed to give
students varied opportunities to develop their character strengths.
As part of the recruitment process, all potential staff are asked why
they want to work at a 'school of character' (Jubilee Centre n.d.-c)
and what they will contribute to the Enrichment programme, which
forms part of their core working hours.

The Year 7 (age 11–12) programme is loosely based around children
finding their place within their community. When the school was
set up, drawing in children from four diverse areas ('nodes') across
the city, it quickly became apparent that many children rarely travel
outside their own neighbourhood, so in Year 7, one of the activities
they do is to go to each other's nodes and explore the sounds, people,
smells, shops, and so on. At the end of this experience, children
write poems that are then published. Other activities include taking
part in community projects – for example, volunteering, cleaning up
parks and singing in old people's homes – and experiencing a 'thank
you café' where they learn to make 'afternoon tea' and serve this to
their parents. Parents from all four nodes are brought in so they can
mix. Another activity involves children discovering different parts of
the University of Birmingham.

In Year 8 (age 12–13), the focus of taught Enrichment is on
children developing their own character, so they have topics such as
'spiritually me' (they visit six places of worship in the area), 'musically
me' (they experience playing instruments from different cultures),
'physically me' (they try out different physical activities – this is

---

1   PSHCE: Personal, social, health and citizenship education. SRE: Sex and relationships
     education. CEIAG: Careers education, information and guidance.
2   PLAD: Personal Learning and Development Programme at UoB School, which includes
     all elements of the taught Character Education curriculum.

linked to the University of Birmingham and they use their facilities for this), and 'my story' (where they explore their own lives through the medium of dramatic performance).

Year 9 students (age 13–14) begin to develop their sense of purpose. Every pupil is funded by the university to participate in the Duke of Edinburgh Award,[3] which they begin preparing for in Year 9. Year 9 students also volunteer with Years 7 and 8, and start thinking about their future careers. Head of School Rebecca Tigue told me a lovely story from a Year 9 Duke of Edinburgh hike in the Peak District. It was extremely cold, there were snow drifts in the mountains, and the ground was so sodden that the children's tents started sliding down the hill halfway through the night. Rebecca was with a group of 'townie boys' and was astounded when one of the boys looked at the landscape and said it was one of the most beautiful things he'd ever seen. He then said:

How can I live my life so I can live somewhere like this?

Year 9 boy at UoB School

In Year 10 (age 14–15) the theme is 'me and my global community', where students explore politics, sociology, psychology and oracy, developing their sense of place in the world and learning to articulate and share their views.

If staff want to cover a topic that doesn't really fit, as long as it helps students develop character, the school supports them in finding a way to make it fit. The school also has a number of links with corporate partners and therefore incorporates any elements that those partners can offer to enhance students' learning. For example, students can now get an engineering qualification as part of their Enrichment programme due to the school's partnership with a large national construction firm.

3   www.dofe.org/do/what

Character taught through a bespoke Character Education curriculum

The taught character curriculum at UoB School is constantly evolving and is different for each year group. Year 7 (age 11–12), for example, have a curriculum based on Andrew Moffat's book about inclusion and equality (Moffat 2017, see Further Reading), which allows them to have highly challenging conversations in safe spaces and teaches them the character strengths of tolerance, compassion and empathy. Where Year 7 pupils learn the vocabulary of character, Year 8 pupils learn the practice by looking at role models and society. In Year 9, they are currently working through *Project Wayfinder* (see Chapter 8). Year 10 (age 14–15) do not have discrete character lessons, but Character Education is delivered through assemblies and tutor times. There is a lead tutor for each year group in school to ensure consistency of Character Education throughout tutor periods in the school.

Other examples of taught Positive Education

In the USA, Breakthrough Magnet School South in Connecticut has experienced tremendous growth in its mindfulness training. The school's social workers learnt about mindfulness 11 years ago and started teaching this to individual children at the school. This then grew to mindfulness clubs and now the whole school receives mindfulness training. At New Canaan Country School (also in the USA), School Psychologist Rebecca Comizio teaches pre-K to fourth grade pupils (age 3–10) executive skills (e.g. organizing their thinking and their time, awareness of their own strengths and limitations, goal-setting, self-monitoring and evaluating). The school counsellor works with teachers and pupils in fifth to ninth grade (age 10–15) on these executive skills as well as teaching a life skills curriculum designed to help them see themselves as adults.

At Kings Langley School in the UK, students are taught about resilience in their PSHE[4] lessons, based on the Penn Resilience

---

4   PSHE: Personal, social, health and economic education.

Programme,[5] which all teachers have been trained in. PSHE curriculum time has been doubled and class sizes halved at the school to accommodate Character Education and ensure themes can be more thoroughly explored. In every year group, national and international news items are discussed through the lens of character, with much debate around the topics and character strengths.

Kti Dossot runs Positive Education courses in higher-education institutions in France. In one such organization, for example, she works with 20-year-old students at the start of the academic year, running Appreciative Inquiry-style[6] strengths workshops to encourage them to envisage their future based on their own happiness/well-being, rather than parental or societal expectations. In another institution, she runs a week covering topics such as assertiveness and positive relationships. Additionally, the organization that originally brought her in to run an Appreciative Inquiry process has now brought her back to run workshops and courses on well-being and Positive Psychology.

At Sunmarke School in Dubai, all pupils from Year 1 (age 5) until they leave school at 19 years of age have 40 minutes per week of Positive Education lessons, where they are taught about Positive Psychology principles such as PERMA (Seligman 2012) and character strengths. Year 7 (age 11–12) is always a challenging year when children transition from primary to secondary education. Having looked at data from the previous academic year, Katrina Mankani noticed children displayed high levels of anxiety, so she introduced an off-curriculum 'relationship week' to start off the year, which gives children time and space – through workshops delivered in a game-like environment – to learn about conflict resolution and active-constructive responding, for example. The outcome of this intervention was that, whereas there had been 27 recorded cases of anxiety the previous year, after the introduction of this activity week, there were none. One minor conflict was recorded in the

---

5   https://guidebook.eif.org.uk/programme/penn-resilience-programme-uk-implementation-in-primary-school

6   See Al Commons n.d.; Cooperrider, Whitney and Stavros 2003; Hall and Hammond n.d.; Srivastava and Cooperrider 1990.

playground, which was immediately resolved through a restorative justice conference delivered by the children, with no further issues arising.

Flora Barton, Headteacher at Crowmarsh Gifford Primary School in the UK, feels that a specific well-being and character curriculum, whether delivered by teachers in school or external providers, is essential, especially as many children don't get taught about well-being and character at home. Bringing in external speakers to deliver assemblies to tie in with the school's Purple Learning ethos – for example, talking about their mistakes and what they have learnt from them – gives children real-life examples showing it's OK to make mistakes. Flora told me how beneficial it was to bring me and Elizabeth Wright[7] into the school to run a Positive and Character Education programme with one of her year groups, as it taught children coping and preventative well-being strategies, such as practising gratitude.

Anni Silverdale Poole is an external provider who works in schools in the UK. Her work with children is around prevention of mental health issues. In Years 5 and 6 (age 9–11), she prepares children for transition to senior school; her work also involves teaching children to understand and manage their emotions. She told me about a Year 5 class she was recently teaching where one child, who had previously often been found roaming the city, unwashed and unfed, and frequently got into trouble, shouted, 'Miss, I get it! I make up my own thoughts... I just spotted one being made and stopped it. It was gonna be really bad, too!'

Through Positive Education, the language of emotions and character strengths begins to seep into everyday life inside and outside of school. This impact of a Positive Education curriculum can be seen at the Berlin Brandenburg International School in Germany. Elke Paul's son attends the school, so his friends, who are also students there, are often at her house. Recently, a group of Year 10 (age 15–16) boys were playing 'Dungeons and Dragons' at her house and, to her delight, she overheard them using the

---

7   co-author of *Character Toolkit for Teachers* (Roberts and Wright 2018).

language of character strengths as part of their game. Often, Years 10, 11 or 12 (age 15–18) students now come into her office and tell her spontaneously if they are suffering from exam stress and need some support with some mindfulness breathing exercises. They understand this helps them, so they actively seek it out when they need it. She also recently ran a relaxation yoga class with a whole Year 10 (age 15–16) cohort of approximately 150 students, and it worked very well.

■ KEY TAKE-AWAYS

1. As well as being *caught*, character can and needs to be *taught* explicitly.

2. Well-being and happiness strategies also need to be taught to children, rather than relying on children absorbing them throughout their time at school.

3. Positive Education lessons need to cover prevention of mental health issues as well as how to manage issues if they do arise.

4. Positive Education can be delivered in a variety of ways, and can be taught by teachers or external specialists.

Chapter 10

EMBEDDED WELL-BEING/CHARACTER LEARNING

You can't capture the beautiful things that happen in Enrichment.

Rebecca Tigue

According to White (2016), well-being is taught in all aspects of school life, not just classrooms. Arthur *et al.* (2015) make a similar case for character development, which they say should be at the core of 'all subjects and all school activities involving every member of school staff'. Schools can teach children positive habits to develop their character strengths, well-being and mental health in subtle, embedded ways in addition to explicit Positive Psychology and Character Education lessons. This includes well-being and character learning in academic subject lessons, in co-curricular activities, in sports activities and from role modelling by adults and other children. In his research, Kristjánsson (2012) found that over 70 percent of teachers believe virtues to be 'caught' and see themselves as 'character role models', a view that is shared by the Department for Education (2017); according to its report, student–staff relationships are paramount and staff need to be models for the strengths they want to develop in students. This role modelling is what the Jubilee Centre for Character and Virtues (2017) describes as 'caught' character.

Positive Education embedded in the academic curriculum

> They don't need a well-being policy because it's built in. It's just there. It just is.

Adele Bates

Adele Bates, who spent a month in Finland in 2019 learning about their education system, told me that well-being is so integral to education there that it doesn't require a separate policy. The national core curriculum mentions 'underlying values', 'school culture', 'motivation and joy of learning' and 'knowledge and skills needed in life'.[1] Its 'transversal competencies' include 'thinking and learning to learn', 'cultural competence, interaction and self-expression', 'taking care of oneself and managing daily life', and 'participation, involvement and building a sustainable future'; all these are elements of Positive Education. The national core curriculum does not prescribe how subjects are taught, but does require teachers and schools to ensure that the 'transversal competencies' are covered. This is similar to how the pillars of the Icelandic national curriculum guides work (see 'Spotlight 3'). Adele spoke to an Arts teacher who told her that he meets with lots of other Arts teachers and they look, together, at how they can interpret the curriculum in their classrooms. For example, he created a wheel of four areas of focus for his lessons; one area was 'how are we connected with others through art?'

One way the 'transversal competencies' of the core curriculum are seen in Finnish education is through assessment. Finnish children don't take any standardized tests until they are 16 years old, though of course teachers still do class tests as needed, but they also assess children through assignments designed to encourage critical and reflective thinking and independent learning. Students are also often assessed on their engagement with classwork and participating in group work and debate. Adele stressed, however,

---

1   www.oph.fi/english/curricula_and_qualifications/basic_education/curricula_2014

that there is a myth that all Finnish teaching is highly progressive and very different to, say, teaching in the UK. She told me that in terms of everyday classroom practice, it was exactly the same; she saw some great 'chalk and talk' lessons, and some rubbish ones, and some 'amazing project-based' learning, and some rubbish lessons taught that way. The difference is that each teacher has the freedom to explore what their classroom needs.

Rebecca Comizio, School Psychologist at New Canaan Country School in the USA, told me embedding the school's *mission skills*[2] into the academic curriculum allows for richer academic lessons that promote higher-order thinking, self-reflection and deeper classroom discussions. She also explained that these correlate with measurable outcomes such as attendance, academic grades and standardized test scores.

Another example of Positive Education embedded in the subjects' curriculum comes from Sunmarke School in Dubai. Katrina Mankani, Director of Positive Education, told me about a Year 1 lesson (age 5–6) where the teacher was discussing the story of Alice in Wonderland with the children. The children then imagined their own wonderland and the teacher asked them to name the character strengths of the heroes in the story. One child said 'self-control'; the teacher asked him to elaborate, and he said, 'Because in my world there are so many sweets that if he doesn't have any self-control, he will eat them all!'

Dan Morrow, CEO of the Woodland Academy Trust in the UK, told me that subjects are merely a transaction for what we're trying to do, which is to allow children to fulfil their dreams.

> Curriculum is a structural framework. Curriculum is people. Curriculum is relationships. Curriculum is spiritual. And therefore, the idea that it is just a book or a folder is absolutely incorrect. A book can do so much, but it will not lead to dreams being fulfilled.
>
> Dan Morrow

---

2   www.countryschool.net/about/mission-skills

Positive Education embedded in other school activities

Geelong Grammar School's Timbertop campus in Australia (see 'Spotlight 1'), presents students with many embedded opportunities for well-being and character development.

> Everywhere there's evidence of overcoming, of persistence, of banding together and collaborating to overcome challenge.
>
> Rhiannon McGee

Head of Positive Education at Geelong Grammar School, Rhiannon McGee, told me that there is no better teacher than experience, but one of the challenges Positive Education faces is that you are teaching concepts, practices and skills out of context. You try very hard to create a context to make that experience authentic, but there is nothing better than that 'scaffolded experience' where students are pushed out of their comfort zone and learn what they are capable of; that's what Timbertop does. Geelong teach much of their Positive Education in an integrated way through teaching of core skills and giving students experiences in areas such as philanthropy and social justice, particularly in the senior years after Timbertop. They do, however, also still have explicit Positive Education lessons to complement this embedded work.

At Lancot Challenger Academy in the UK, the entire teaching methodology and curriculum delivery is character-focused and cross-curricular. Character is embedded into all learning and forms the central core of the school's ethos.

Also in the UK, the Odyssey Trust's ethos is in line with the position of the Jubilee Centre for Character and Virtues (2017) that character can be both taught and caught. Every aspect of the curriculum is related back to character. For example, the Trust's Director of Character Education and Well-being and Assistant Headteacher at Townley Grammar School, Fabian de Fabiani, told me of a conversation he overheard between a boy and his Maths teacher at King Henry School. The boy questioned why he needed to learn Maths. 'I'm going to work for my dad!' he said. His dad is a self-employed tradesperson, so the teacher explained that people in that trade need to understand angles and calculate invoices, for which he will need Maths, but also that he needs common sense to run his business; phronesis, otherwise known as 'practical wisdom' (Jubilee Centre 2017) is one of the central tenets of Character Education. Much of the focus when developing the academic curriculum, co-curricular activities and other opportunities for character development at the Odyssey Trust goes on what students need to know when they leave. The schools are there to support students in developing a sense of purpose and accompany them along a part of the journey to get there. At Townley Grammar School, for example, pupils in Years 8 and 9 (age 12–14) have the option to take a course in International Relations. Students also look at current affairs issues; so, for example, there was recently a whole topic where students created their own 'fake news' stories so they'd be better able to develop their critical thinking skills and recognize these so-called news items when they see them.

Specialists can support schools in embedding Positive Education into the academic curriculum. As a School Psychologist in a school with a strong Positive Education focus, Rebecca Comizio has been given much autonomy at New Canaan Country School. She works with teachers and administrators to set the social and emotional goals for each grade so teachers can then integrate these into their subject curriculum, and is able to support them by delivering assemblies to whole year groups or assist teachers in integrating Positive Education into their lesson plans. She has been in her role for a couple of years now and told me it takes a little time to bring everyone on board with the vision of what Positive Education could be, but the school has now reached a point where some teachers want to bring in mindfulness, or 'catching children doing great stuff', or integrating the school's mission skills.

Positive Education can also be embedded in non-academic school activities. At the University of Birmingham (UoB) School in the UK, Enrichment sessions are one of the ways for children to develop character. In Chapter 9, I gave examples of the way this is formally taught; here I will give examples of how it is 'caught' (Jubilee Centre for Character and Virtues 2017, n.d.-a, n.d.-c).

For Friday afternoon Enrichment sessions, school and university staff, parents, and corporate partners can offer any activities they like. Children choose activities which they do in five blocks of eight to nine weeks. The only stipulation is that once students have chosen an activity, they have to stick to it, as this helps build their character strengths of grit, resilience and curiosity. This also encourages them to be brave and do things they want to do, rather than just doing what their friends are doing.

> We finish Friday with an hour and a half of pure joy, fun and loveliness!
>
> Rebecca Tigue

Rebecca Tigue, Head of School, told me the benefits of this activity are immense. Children from different year groups work together and see staff in a different light, outside of their formal roles in school. Some groups also have Year 12 and 13 (age 16–18) supervisors, giving students the opportunity to develop leadership skills and to role model behaviour and character strengths for the younger children.

Activities on the day of my visit to the school included:

- 'Girl Dreamer': This is delivered by an external provider to increase the confidence of young girls. They meet inspirational women from business, develop their own personal brand and create a 'Sisterhood Manifesto'. One girl doing this activity told me that they talked about topics around growing up, being a girl, role models, how to deal with various situations in life, going to college, career choices and more. She said it gave them an understanding that life isn't a straight path, and also told me that it was great the activity wasn't delivered by a teacher.

- Knitting club: I spoke to some students doing this activity. One girl had never knitted before and didn't think she could knit a scarf, but was now making great progress. She told me that she was making the scarf for her mum and that she found knitting very relaxing as she doesn't think of anything when

she knits. She said she would likely continue knitting outside
of school and that her family is now putting in requests!

- One boy, who was learning to do magic tricks and delighted
  in showing off his newly acquired skills, had previously done
  rugby, football and parkour running. He said he liked the
  opportunity to try out different sports. In previous school
  years, he had taken trips to the University of Birmingham and
  learnt to do stop-motion animation.

I didn't expect school to be like that!

Student at UoB School

Ofsted[3] rated the school as 'good' overall in its first inspection in
2018 and the Ofsted report refers to the positive impact Character
Education has made on children's personal development and on
their mental health.

Sunmarke School and Regent International School in Dubai
(Fortes Education) provide many opportunities for children to learn
about well-being and character development outside the classroom,
such as the Duke of Edinburgh Award and school trips. Within
the school environment, the Fortes team of educators has created
routine activities to put Positive Education into practice, such as:

- Peer counselling: This gives students the opportunity to talk to
  a peer rather than an adult. They have peer counsellors across
  all age groups from primary to secondary. Peer counsellors
  receive two weeks of training and are then able to devise their
  own plan of how and where counselling happens. Solutions
  and actions are agreed between peer counsellors and the
  students they counsel. Peer counsellors have meaning and
  purpose, and are able to develop many character strengths
  such as empathy, leadership and kindness.

---

3   Ofsted: Office for Standards in Education. This is the UK government's schools inspection
     body for schools in England.

- Sports Heroes Academy: Secondary school students are trained as junior sports coaches to become buddies to SEND[4] children. Children come to the school from all over the United Arab Emirates and the academy is run free of charge. They currently have 240 participating students – 120 volunteers and 120 SEND children. Additionally, there are volunteer teachers and coaches. This academy helps students develop character strengths such as leadership, empathy, resilience and compassion.

Even in schools where a whole school Positive Education ethos has not been adopted, it is still possible for individual teachers to embed this into their own lessons. Paul Bateson told me how he embedded Positive Education into his tutor periods – for example, by doing the tutor time spelling test on words related to kindness. He also worked with the Media Studies students in the school, who produced a weekly 'reflections' video where students and teachers reflected on things that had happened during the week; he asked them to create one of those videos with the #itsnicetobenice theme.

Well-being and character learnt from role models

Eleanor Ellis Bryant, Subject Leader for Religious Studies and Staff Governor at the UoB School, told me that Enrichment gives teachers an opportunity to have a different relationship with the children. For example, in one session she had a conversation with an adopted child about what it feels like to be adopted; and in another, a girl opened up to her about her controlling boyfriend, and she could support the student through the situation without being in a formal 'teacher' role. She said that they 'get to chat about everyday life and it enhances classroom relationships'. The opportunity for students to see teachers outside of the classroom context also paves the way for teachers to role model numerous character strengths and positive relationships.

---

4   SEND: Special Educational Needs and Disabilities.

As we saw in Chapter 7, the UoB School's building has been designed with Character Education in mind, and that includes providing every opportunity for children to develop character by watching role models. There are staff work bases with glass walls at the end of every corridor, so pupils can see what working life looks like for the adults in the school – from hard work and concentration to coffee breaks. At the heart of the school, there is a large atrium to enable staff and pupils to eat together. This space is also used by Year 12 and 13 students (age 16–18) as a study area when they are not in lessons, providing academic role models for the younger pupils through the display of character strengths such as hard work, perseverance and curiosity.

Character can be caught from role models in a more deliberate and overt manner, too. In my training sessions, I always encourage teachers to work with students to identify character role models – whether these are from the sports/politics/music celebrity world or from their own family/friendship/school and wider community circles. Once these role models are identified, students can create and display posters with their key character strengths as a reminder of the strengths students may want to emulate at various times in their lives. I recently discovered *Amazing People Schools*,[5] an interactive web-based resource for schools that uses the stories behind contemporary and historical names from the world of politics, science, art and more to allow children to learn about character from role models. Whilst this can be built into a specific Character Education curriculum, the website is designed to also enable teachers to embed Character Education into the academic curriculum. I have met the team and they are passionate about supporting the development of character and well-being in schools. This resource is a great example, along with *Lyfta* (see Chapter 12), of how technology and story-telling can be brought into the classroom and wider school as part of a whole school approach to Positive Education.

---

5   www.amazingpeopleschools.com

▒ KEY TAKE-AWAYS

1. For a whole school approach to Positive Education, it is useful to have multiple ways to embed well-being and character learning throughout the school's activities.

2. Embedding can happen in subject lessons, through enrichment and other non-academic activities, and via role modelling of well-being-enhancing behaviours and desirable character traits.

3. Role models can be adults or other children.

Chapter 11

TARGETED INTERVENTIONS

We ensure there is a boat that can take children back to the shore when they're drowning.

Katrina Mankani

As we've seen in previous chapters, Positive Education interventions and programmes tend to be applied to all students in a school or in a class or year group, but whole school Positive Education also requires a targeted approach for more vulnerable children. According to Seligman *et al.* (2019), providing focused evidence-based interventions is one answer to the deepening crisis in children's mental health. Public Health England (2015), Lopes *et al.* (2013) and Stirling and Emery (2016) also recommend aiming interventions at specific pupils who need them the most, in addition to a wider whole school provision for all pupils.

Targeted interventions for children

One of the things Flora Barton, Headteacher at Crowmarsh Gifford Primary School in the UK, did when she joined the school was to introduce a full-time home–school link worker to support children. They can go to her if they have any issues or concerns so she can help get them be ready to learn.

> A child getting into our Trust has an invisible backpack. Our job is to unpack that for them.
>
> Dan Morrow

Dan Morrow, CEO of the Woodland Academy Trust in the UK, told me the story of one pupil with asylum-seeker status who had no spoken English when they joined one of the schools in the Trust. The strong pastoral focus and holistic approach in the Trust helped this pupil 'unpick and unpack' their traumatic experiences and the 'toxins adults had put into their life'. Now, after three years in the UK, this pupil has secured a place at a grammar school[1] and they 'will go there smiling'.

Adele Bates told me that the Finnish education system is set up to offer extensive individual support to every student that needs it. In her blog (Bates 2019), Adele explains that every school has a counsellor who meets with every student regularly. Additionally, class sizes are small (the maximum, by law, is 22 students) and schools are not allowed to stream students by academic ability. This is possible because each school has a strong support team. By law, there has to be one SEND[2] teacher – educated to at least Master's level – for every 200 students, in addition to classroom assistants. If there is a concern about a child, there is a three-tier support system: Level one is general support such as contacting parents/carers and discussing the child with other teachers to investigate what the issues are and how the school can support the child. The next level of support involves the school's social worker looking at underlying issues. If that isn't enough, more intense support is offered by the school psychiatrist or counsellor. Adele told me that what is so wonderful is that the pastoral side of education is taken care of by people who are well-being professionals. She said that she has seen 'the most nurturing, most differentiated teaching' in SEND classes, where each teacher adapted their support to provide exactly what children needed, which even included supporting parents with CV writing and job-hunting!

---

1   In England and Northern Ireland, a grammar school is a state-funded academically selective school. Children need to sit and pass the '11-plus' exam to secure a place.
2   SEND: Special educational needs and disabilities.

School social workers and psychiatrists/psychologists are linked into the city's resources, so when they do spot an issue, they can act fast. For example, if they request an emergency session via the Finnish equivalent of CAMHS,[3] this will happen within 24 hours. Standard referrals take about a week. This is in sharp contrast to UK timescales, where many children are not offered support from CAMHS at all and waiting times can be up to six months for a first appointment and as long as 42 weeks before treatment starts (Frith 2016).

Back in the UK, much of the Positive Education work at Lessness Heath Primary School has gone into building more trust between staff, staff and pupils, and the school and families. Kelly Hannaghan, Well-Being Leader, told me about one young girl who used to go into school crying every day because she thought she was fat and ugly. As a result, she was seeking attention with negative behaviour and had a difficult relationship with her teachers. Kelly described her as a 'very bright young lady that wasn't reaching her full potential; she was really struggling with some overwhelming feelings'. The school has a robust monitoring and measuring system for children's well-being and uses a four-tier approach for early intervention: Teachers are skilled at asking mental health and well-being questions and identifying issues, the school can offer emotional literacy support, Kelly provides therapeutic play sessions, and ultimately the school can make a referral to CAMHS. Because of this, they were able to quickly identify that there was a problem with the young girl. This pupil had severe issues with confidence and self-esteem and her family was on a long-term safeguarding plan, but the situation wasn't improving. The parents had a difficult relationship with their daughter and at times found it overwhelming and unbearable to be with her. The school offered a package of support. They supported teachers in dealing with her behaviour in the classroom through teacher and child therapeutic sessions and the mum was invited onto the 'family matters' programme where she learnt to be open about her own challenges. They also did a lot of work

---

3   CAMHS: Child and adolescent mental health services; part of the UK's National Health System.

with the mum around what lay beneath the child's behaviour. The child herself had therapeutic play sessions and interventions from CAMHS. Kelly told me the 'magical element' is that the outcome for the family was fantastic. They have been off the safeguarding plan for about 18 months and they're thriving. The mother and daughter have an amazing relationship. The mother continues to engage with the family matters programme.

You've saved my relationship with my daughter.

Mother of a young girl at Lessness Heath Primary School

The mother is very grateful for the support and is now an active member of the 'change' team involving staff, families, local community members and police. She's actively campaigned for the school around mental health days, and said that the help she received and the work she's committed to has been life-changing.

Kelly also told me another story about a family who had adopted a child but had not received much support from the adoption service. The child had experienced lots of trauma and had attachment and behavioural issues, and the family felt very isolated. The school provided extensive support for the child and family, which made a huge difference.

Coming to school is like winning the lottery.

Family of a child at Lessness Heath Primary School

I introduced you to Lessness Heath Primary School's therapy dog, Lola, in Chapter 7. Lola has dedicated 'Lola Leaders', who are amongst the most vulnerable children in the school. Their role is to walk Lola to the school gate, accompanied by an adult. This offers opportunities to 'walk and talk' and develop positive relationships with adults in the school. It has been a highly successful programme and the attendance of those pupils has improved as a result. Katy O'Connor, Headteacher, told me that Lola is having a great impact on children who are on the autism spectrum. Lola lives in her office and the children often come in and say hello to her. Katy can immediately see a change in their demeanor and anxiety levels.

Another school in the UK with a therapy dog is Townley Grammar School. Additionally, the school has expert support from two school counsellors and, thanks to their strong focus on mental health, they are adept at identifying when students need outside help. They have a significant number of students who need outside support (e.g. from CAMHS) and were one of the first schools to join the 'Time to Change'[4] mental health awareness campaign to combat the stigma around mental health. Sixty-five students in the school are well-being ambassadors who have received 'mental health first aid'[5] and coaching training so they can offer peer-to-peer support to other students.

At Fortes Education in Dubai, targeted interventions come under the 'responsive tier' of Positive Education. They have counsellors and psychologists, including a positive psychologist at Sunmarke School, who can take care of students' well-being when they need additional support. Additionally, all teachers are trained in mental health first response. Students participate in an annual survey that helps identify children who are at risk so school can immediately plan an intervention. One example of targeted interventions is the use of restorative justice at both Fortes Education schools (Regent International School and Sunmarke). This is something the teams have worked hard to establish and embed; Katrina Mankani delivered an inspiring presentation on this topic at the International Positive Education Network (IPEN) Festival in Texas in 2018. When restorative justice is well established in a school, it can help resolve even the most complex of issues and contributes to the overall Positive Education ethos. For example, one Year 6 (age 10–11) child approached another to offer to do their homework in exchange for money. Both children got caught; thanks to the restorative justice process, they were able to acknowledge their mistakes and decide on how to best move forward. The money was returned, apology letters were written and they fully understood the issue in a way they may not have done if they had simply been punished for their actions.

---

4   www.time-to-change.org.uk
5   https://mhfaengland.org

Not all targeted interventions arise out of a major issue requiring multiple support mechanisms and referrals. Rebecca Comizio, Psychologist at New Canaan Country School in the USA told me the lovely story of a little girl in first grade (age 6–7) who was afraid of thunderstorms. There had been a lot of severe weather and this was on the news a lot. Rebecca started off with some cognitive behavioural therapy techniques by talking about 'thinking like a scientist', considering how dangerous Connecticut thunderstorms really are, how many of them have caused serious problems, who is in charge of making sure the school buildings are safe and so on. At the end, she told the girl about the expression 'every cloud has a silver lining'. She explained the metaphor to the little girl, who drew a beautiful picture to represent it. The next day, she came in, all excited:

Mrs Comizio, I found the silver lining!

First grade pupil at New Canaan Country School

She told Rebecca this beautiful story about how, when it had rained one day, she'd been really nervous, but she'd found a cosy spot in her bedroom and settled in there with her cat. She got a flashlight and put a blanket over herself and the cat and read a book to the cat. 'That was the silver lining, because if it hadn't been rainy and dark, I might not have taken that time to sit and read to him!'

That story, her little face, the joy she felt instead of the fear… It will stay in my heart forever!

Rebecca Comizio

Targeted interventions for staff

Whole school Positive Education includes ensuring that the well-being and character development of staff are provided for.

Lola, the therapy dog at Lessness Heath Primary School, has had an unexpected impact on staff. Kelly Hannaghan spent a lot of time talking to the school's cleaners. Although they are employed directly by the school, they felt disconnected from the rest of the staff. Then, one day, they excitedly told Kelly they'd found what they needed: Lola! They had found that talking to her and stroking her when they were at work helped them immensely. Kelly told me that people's needs are not always immediately apparent, but that it's important never to give up and to keep asking people what they need.

Dan Morrow, CEO of the Woodland Academy Trust, feels strongly about the need to support staff and adopts the same approach with them as he does with children. You will find some beautiful quotes from him on this topic in Chapter 1, under 'Staff well-being'. He told me how he regularly tells staff: 'I expect one thing only – for you to be smiling because you are enjoying your work.'

> If you are not smiling, I assume someone hasn't done what they need to do to allow you to be your best self today.
>
> Dan Morrow

Patrick Ottley-O'Connor, Executive Headteacher at North Liverpool Academy (UK) and Education Consultant and Coach, told me that because of his approach to mental health and well-being, staff share what goes on in their lives with him and with each other. In his current school he runs a weekly session of 'sharing by staff for staff', where staff secretly nominate each other for having been kind or supportive. Nominees are then selected at random to win wine or chocolates. They can ask why they have been nominated, but will not find out who nominated them. The nomination reason is also not shared publicly. This process brings heart-breaking and heart-warming stories to Patrick's attention, which is a great way for him to know what is going on in the lives of his staff and know who needs additional support from time to time.

For example, when one teacher's mum died, while the teacher was on leave, all other staff stepped in and did all of that teacher's marking so that when the teacher returned, there was no need to catch up. Through this initiative, Patrick found out not only about female members of staff who had suffered miscarriages, but about male members of staff whose partners had suffered a miscarriage, which is something that is rarely talked about, so the men usually suffer in silence. Because Patrick was aware of these bereavements, he was able to – confidentially and with prior permission – put teachers who had suffered miscarriages or whose partners had suffered miscarriages in touch with each other for mutual support. As a result of this, the staff set up a self-perpetuating support group that others have since joined.

Patrick says that sometimes people 'just need a lift'. For example, the school has also been able to support staff members who have faced financial difficulties.

KEY TAKE-AWAYS

1. In a whole school approach to Positive Education, targeted interventions are required to support individual children and teachers when they need it, in addition to the well-being and character lessons and the embedded learning that happens in school.

2. Targeted interventions can be huge and involve external providers, or be little things that make a big difference.

Chapter 12

ENGAGEMENT AND REACH

It takes the synchronicity of parents, teachers, the counsellor, etc. all using genuine, specific praise and guidance, sending the same message at the same time. It's the synchronicity that makes it powerful.

Rebecca Comizio

In this chapter, I will be rounding off the concept of whole school Positive Education. We'll look at how stakeholder ownership of, and engagement with, initiatives, involving and supporting the community, and parental involvement are essential to making Positive Education truly 'whole school'. There is some overlap between the three areas, but for ease of reading I have separated the chapter into the three distinct sub-topics: ownership, community and parents.

Ownership

Weare (2015) stresses all key stakeholders, including children and their parents/carers, need to be engaged and committed to a school's well-being initiatives for them to succeed. Waters *et al.* (2015) also support a collaborative approach and highlight the benefits of using an Appreciative Inquiry process (AI Commons n.d.; Srivastava and Cooperrider 1990) to help promote that sense of ownership.

In Appreciative Inquiry, representatives of all stakeholder groups celebrate past achievements and recognize the strengths used and satisfactions gained from those achievements, before applying them to move forward and set about achieving their dreams for the future. This is the next step that Elke Paul, Positive Education Consultant at Berlin Brandenburg International School in Germany, wants to take there. She intends to create a student and staff implementation team, hold an Appreciative Inquiry summit and then move forward with the decisions arising from it. She describes the next phase as 'moving from the what to the how'.

Morgan (2017) also underlines how important it is for staff, parents and the wider community to be fully involved and to role model character strengths for the children. White (2016) highlights how initiatives driven from the bottom up are more durable than ones originating from the top through policy.

Part of the longer-term development plan and vision the Odyssey Trust has for King Henry School in the UK is to reduce the amount of teacher-led guidance, so that students can take more ownership over their self-regulation and sense of purpose, learning to make ethical choices. Additionally, the aim is to have collaboration between staff and students in developing policies, which will generate more buy-in from the ground up.

Ownership of initiatives can take many forms. At Crowmarsh Gifford Primary School (UK), for example, there is a strong emphasis on openly talking about mistakes made and the growth that can come from those. Everyone in the school community, from Headteacher Flora Barton to the staff, children and parents, engage in the #BePhenomenal practice and sharing their mistakes (see Chapter 7).

Flora gave me a personal example of this. The summer before she took up her post at the school, she wrote her Master's dissertation. That October, she found out she wouldn't pass her Master's as the dissertation wasn't strong enough. She resubmitted with minimal changes and without speaking to her supervisor as she was short on time, so later that year, in December, she failed again. She told no one aside from her family. She eventually reworked it and gained a distinction. Last year, she felt like a fraud for not having shared this with the school community. During a staff meeting, she told all her staff the full story, then ran an assembly about it for the children. She said it felt really good to share the story; she was no longer hiding. She felt it was important to share how the failure had been a great opportunity for growth. Children talk to her about that example a lot; it's good for them to see that adults make mistakes, too, and that they are still learning.

Sometimes one person can start a ripple effect that turns into a big wave. Paul Bateson found that, after he introduced the #itsnicetobenice project in his school with a group of dedicated students from the school council, other teachers began to take ownership of this and to use the hashtag in e-mails. Students did spontaneous acts of kindness; for example, when one teacher broke a mug during drama rehearsals, a student came in with a new mug for the teacher the next day.

Patrick Ottley-O'Connor talked to me about how taking ownership can impact positively on the mental health of staff and on the school culture. When he went into a previous school as Executive Headteacher, the school had been in 'special measures' for two years, but the culture changed at such a pace that the school came out of special measures so fast the Ofsted[1] report was delayed for three months to be reviewed and discussed at the highest level; it seemed impossible for a school's culture to have changed so quickly. Patrick said this arose out of the sharing practices he introduced (see Chapter 11) that built trust between staff. He places great onus on ownership of one's own problems and mental health, while offering all the support, coaching and recognition that staff need. According to Patrick, ownership is a great way to build mental health and well-being, resilience and character.

In Finland, teachers have a lot of autonomy, which gives them full ownership over their time and their well-being. Adele Bates told

---

1   Ofsted is the UK government's inspection organization for schools in England. 'Special measures' is a rating given to schools by Ofsted when they are deemed to require extensive intervention and support due to not meeting requirements. They are inspected regularly and staff can be replaced by an appointed executive committee.

me that one teacher she stayed with in Finland doesn't teach until lunchtime on two days a week, so that time is her own. She can work from home, use it to meet parents, do some marking, or have a lie-in, walk the dog or read a book. This has a huge impact on teacher well-being. Children also have individual timetables and if they're not in lessons, they don't have to be in school. They are given responsibility and autonomy from an early age, which develops their character strengths.

Even the youngest children can take ownership over initiatives that matter to them and develop their well-being and character strengths. Julie Goldstein, Principal at the Breakthrough Magnet School South in the USA, told me a beautiful story that would equally be at home in the 'community' section, below. A group of three 7–8-year-old children in second and third grade wanted other children less fortunate than them to be happy. They came up with their own community service idea, set up a donation station and collected close to 200 toys, which were then delivered to the local children's medical centre. They ran the project by holding a weekly community meeting, enlisted the help of their peers and did it all without fanfare.

Rebecca Tigue, Head of School at the University of Birmingham (UoB) School (UK) told me a lovely anecdote about a boy who, on the last day of term, appeared in her office and apologized for not having got her a present but gave her a single chocolate.

> I kept my last chocolate for you because it's really important to show gratitude!
>
> Student at UoB School

Later I was lucky enough to meet this boy. Rebecca told him she'd told me about the chocolate, and he was beaming with joy!

Community

The importance of fostering positive relationships between school, students, families and the wider community is underscored in Thomson (2010). According to Sergiovanni (1994), communities have principles and morals in common. Roffey (2012) calls this the school's 'social capital' (p.146), reflected in the ability to depend on each other, trust each other, feel a sense of kinship and share a sense of morality. According to her, governments are taking notice of social capital and realizing the potential for this to have a positive impact on outcomes for all children, but particularly for children from disadvantaged backgrounds.

One of the guiding principles of the Health Promoting Schools programme in Iceland is that all stakeholders actively participate. Iceland is also a participant in the European Union-funded international research programme UPRIGHT, which is targeted at families, schools and communities.[2]

Supporting the local community

At Crowmarsh Gifford Primary School, serving and supporting the local community is a big part of the school's ethos. For example, Headteacher Flora Barton told me about a 'random acts of kindness' event, where randomly selected children gave flowers and gift tokens to randomly selected (e.g. everyone wearing a scarf) people in town. She said it was wonderful to see people's reactions, and the activity was filmed so that it could then be shared in an assembly with the whole school. In another activity, children went to a local restaurant and made pizzas, which they then delivered to homeless people in Oxford. I could hear the joy in Flora's voice as she told me about the ripple effect these activities caused. Children are now independently modelling the behaviour outside of school.

The #itsnicetobenice project launched by Paul Bateson at his last school captured the imaginations of the students, who soon wanted to do more and decided to undertake some volunteering projects.

> We're supposed to be a Community Academy. What do we do for the community?
>
> Student at Paul Bateson's last school

---

2   www.uprightprogram.eu

They ran a coffee morning in school and invited service users from the Age UK charity, charity volunteers and local care home residents. Staff and students worked together, baking cakes and serving tea/coffee and cake to their visitors. One 100-year-old lady who spent time chatting to a Year 7 (age 11–12) pupil said she was 'buzzing' from the event! After that, the students still wanted to do more, so they got in touch with a local food bank and organized a collection for them. This has carried on in the school since then, even after Paul left. The dedicated group of students also went and volunteered at a local homeless shelter and soup kitchen. They still wanted to do more and asked if they could set up a 'proper charity'. Paul helped them plan this and built it into his lessons, covering various cross-curricular aspects such as designing a logo and writing a mission statement.

Townley Grammar School in the UK has seen the development of a strong ethos of social action. In 2014 they launched a project involving Year 10 students (age 14–15) researching a social issue and local grassroots charities working on it. They then became advocates for one charity by taking part in a competition where they could win a £1000 funding award for the charity. Since then, this has grown into the 'First Give' programme, which runs in over 200 UK schools. Over 800 students at Townley Grammar have participated to date, providing real support to local grassroots organizations while developing their own character alongside practical skills. Many students have carried on working with the charities they represented by volunteering for them in Years 12 and 13 (age 16–18). Fabian de Fabiani gave me an example of one such project. A Group of students identified 'Samuel's Charity', a charity set up by a dad who lost his 8-year-old son to a severe form of leukaemia. One of the boy's dying wishes was for a charity to be set up for children's wards to be less clinical. The students at Townley Grammar School fundraised, but more importantly campaigned to raise awareness. They showed great maturity in how they ran the project and how they wanted to preserve the legacy of the dying child's sense of purpose in the most challenging of circumstances.

For its 75th anniversary year, Lichfield Cathedral School in the UK ran a '75 acts of kindness' project, which included small acts such as thanking the person serving dinner in school and bigger projects in the local community. For example, they made contact with their local community hospital and took some Year 6 and 7 students (age 10–12) to make a garden for them out of a piece of wasteland. Parents helped, two local garden centres donated everything, and over two days the students transformed the space. The school still periodically sends students to tidy up the garden. Jo Owens, Director of Ethical Leadership, told me: 'It was brilliant! It refocused the conversations we were having with parents about children and made it very clear what we value in school.' Parents started e-mailing her not only to tell her about what their own children had done, but about what other children had done for their children!

The school as a community

'Community' can also refer to the school itself. Kelly Hannaghan, Well-Being Leader at Lessness Heath Primary School in the UK, used a lovely phrase when describing the school: 'Our school is a loving, caring community.' This was also reflected in Patrick Ottley-O'Connor's ethos.

> The way we speak to each other doesn't cost a penny.
>
> Patrick Ottley-O'Connor

As this sense of community becomes part of the culture wherever Patrick works, he is not the only person leading initiatives. For example, the Acting Principal at North Liverpool Academy, where Patrick is currently Executive Headteacher, brings in 'bacon butties'[3] for colleagues to thank them for their hard work. She also buys a small present and birthday card for every member of staff's birthday.

At Geelong Grammar School's Timbertop campus in Australia, students undergo a rigorous and challenging year, during which the only contact they have with their families during term-time is by letter. This, combined with the intensity of shared experiences,

---

3   A colloquial term for a bacon sandwich.

bonds the students in strong positive relationships and builds a lasting sense of community.

The wider community

Following the lead from Geelong Grammar School, Elke Paul would like Berlin Brandenburg International School to become a 'lighthouse school' for Positive Education, offering professional development programmes for staff at other schools. Elke already presents the Positive Education work done at Berlin Brandenburg International School at conferences around the world.

Townley Grammar School shares this altruistic outlook and wants to share its knowledge of Character Education with other schools – for example, by hosting character conferences. This sense of community responsibility is the reason why Townley Grammar School took the step of forming the Multi-Academy Trust (MAT)[4] by taking on King Henry School. It was the first time that a grammar school had formed a MAT with a comprehensive school.

At Lessness Heath Primary School, Kelly Hannaghan also takes every opportunity to share the journey the school has been on with other educators by inviting other teachers into the school and running workshops in school and at conferences.

Schools also have a responsibility to provide children with opportunities to become open-minded global citizens and to break down some of the toxic divisive 'them and us' barriers we are seeing around the world. Townley Grammar School has a global committee and runs a global learning programme (Townley Grammar School n.d.) across all year groups. During the research for this book, I discovered Lyfta,[5] an education organization that creates 'immersive human stories'. Serdar Ferit, Lyfta's Co-CEO and Creative Director,

---

4   An academy in England is a school funded by the government but run independently. At the time of writing, around three-quarters of English secondary schools are academies. Because they are not controlled by the local education authority, they are able to set their own curriculum, holiday dates, etc. A Multi-Academy Trust is a group of academies that work closely with each other and have some common governance, usually with a common Chief Executive Officer and governing board.

5   www.lyfta.com

told me that, as documentary film-makers, he and his partner wanted to make documentaries more experiential by inviting viewers into the story. As Serdar had been a teacher for ten years, they eventually tested an immersive story in a school. Children are invited into the personal spaces of people who live different lives to their own. They can look around the spaces, clicking on any items to learn more about them and, when they're ready, they can click on the person, who then tells them their story in a short documentary film. The first time they took this into a school, the children were mesmerized and were able to answer questions in great detail afterwards. The teacher was moved to tears.

Parents

Parents are a key stakeholder group in any school community. Konu and Rimpelä (2002) underline the direct impact that the children's living environments have on the children and their schools. Public Health England (2014) refers to the need for schools to work with families, external providers and the wider school community to enhance children's health and well-being in a consistent manner. Waters *et al.*'s (2015) recommendation goes further, specifying that it is beneficial for schools to train and inform parents through courses and information events.

According to Gary Lewis, Headteacher at Kings Langley School in the UK, most of the research into Character Education now goes into the work schools do with parents. At Kings Langley, all parents go through a Character Education programme to help them overcome what Gary calls 'glasshouse parenting'. The training events take place in a relaxed atmosphere over cheese and wine and, after an initial presentation, parents are given a series of moral dilemmas to discuss. The school runs a number of these evenings so various dilemmas can be explored.

Ultimately the test of good character is 'do you make the right decision?'

Gary Lewis

As Gary explained, it's not all about the decision, as it's not always black or white, but about how you come to the decision. The reflection is important.

Elke Paul also runs cheese and wine nights for parents at Berlin Brandenburg International School. She is in the process of organizing a two-day parent retreat and the format is gaining strong buy-in for Positive Education from the parents. There are strong levels of family engagement with Positive Education at Geelong Grammar School, too, as we explored in 'Spotlight 1'.

When children win a place at Breakthrough Magnet School South in the 'lottery' allocation, parents have to understand and commit to the ethos of the school, working in partnership with teachers. They all have the principal's mobile number and, to embed the parents' commitment to the school's values, all new parents attend a course once a week for a month.

> The world shows us talent and makes it look easy. Kids are inundated! They are comparing themselves to the entire universe of people!
>
> Rebecca Comizio

Rebecca Comizio, Psychologist at New Canaan Country School in the USA, also delivers presentations to parents on relevant topics. For example, she recently gave a talk based on the book *The Self-Driven Child* (Stixrud 2019), sharing the basics of self-determination theory and what that looks like in school, giving parents advice on how to best support their children – for example by not driving back to school to drop off their lunch or sports equipment if they forgot to take it, but letting them learn from the consequences of their actions instead. In her work with parents, Rebecca wants to empower them to give their children the space to develop their character strengths. She firmly believes that if parents and school send a consistent message to children at the same time, this can be incredibly powerful in supporting children's well-being and growth.

Lessness Heath Primary School offers extensive support to parents and they, in turn, get involved and give back to the school community by supporting initiatives and campaigns to help other families. You can read about an example of this in Chapter 11.

◼ KEY TAKE-AWAYS

1. For Positive Education to be at its most effective, all stakeholders need to be committed to it and take ownership over initiatives. Anyone in the school community can drive forward an initiative.

2. Positive Education includes supporting the local community through charity and volunteering projects, growing a stronger sense of community cohesion within the school, and a wider understanding of and support of the wider, global community.

3. Parents need to be involved in the school community and understand, buy into and support the school's Positive Education ethos and initiatives. Equally, Positive Education schools have a responsibility to support students by supporting their families. This includes working with their parents through education events and targeted interventions as needed.

Chapter 13

TURNING DREAMS INTO REALITY

My only dream for children is that they find their dream.

Dan Morrow

In this final chapter, I will summarize the key themes that came out of the responses contributors gave me to three key questions, and will invite you – no, *urge* you – to think about those questions for yourself, *write down* some answers, and then *get to work* to turn your education dreams into reality, because this book is useless if you don't take action!

How does it feel?

The most frequent response to this question was 'proud'. When teachers, school leaders, well-being specialists and other education professionals witness those amazing, heart-warming moments when a child's life, or a family's relationships, or a teacher's well-being is improved before their eyes, they feel justifiably proud: of themselves, of their colleagues, of the children and the families they work with; proud of the hard work, determination and courage that goes into making those moments possible.

As educators, we love our students. When you see someone you love reframe a challenge in a positive way, that feeling is overwhelmingly positive. I feel relieved, hopeful, proud of us as a community, that we were all able to do this and give him what he needed to be his best and proud of himself and continue to move forward. It's a great sense of satisfaction.

Rebecca Comizio

The next-biggest response was one of optimism and hope, which reflects how I feel after spending months doing research and carrying out interviews for this book! Like any movement, it takes time and oh so much effort, but change is coming; change is already happening.

When you take a moment to stop and notice, and realize you are living this change, you are a part of it, you are contributing to it, of course you are bound to feel grateful, which is another theme that emerged. With passion for change, it is perhaps inevitable to also experience some frustration.

Some academies are widget factories. What is the value of a child that should be a Grade 6 Maths getting a Grade 8, when time could be spent on enabling them to learn essential skills instead?

Gary Lewis

It is affirming but also frustrating. This stuff should happen more and everywhere.

Fabian de Fabiani

Other ways people described their emotions included 'passionate', 'motivated', 'energized', 'committed', 'resilient', 'curious', 'happy' and 'excited'.

It's exciting to be part of the big change. Sometimes in the day to day we lose the sense that, in 20 years' time, we can look back at what we've achieved and changed. I'm feeling very optimistic about our movement.

Fabian de Fabiani

This is what I wake up every day for!

Katrina Mankani

It reminded me why I was a teacher! It's not just about teaching my subject, it's about nurturing children and watching them become who they're meant to be and growing into their personalities.

Jo Owens

◼ OVER TO YOU

1. Write down a few notes about three great stories related to well-being or character development that happened in your school.

2. Reflect on how each story made you feel, and write down those feelings.

What strengths do you need?

I asked the people I interviewed what strengths they and their school community used in making the stories they shared with me happen. The list was almost as long as the list of VIA strengths,[1] but a few were mentioned more often than others: Open-mindedness and persistence were those mentioned the most, closely followed by interpersonal skills, resilience, collaboration, leadership and courage. Authenticity, empathy and belief were a close third. Other strengths included gratitude, humour, optimism, love, curiosity and love of learning.

It would therefore appear that in order to grow the Positive Education ethos and initiatives in your school, it is useful to ensure that you and/or your team members and colleagues have those strengths amongst what the VIA Institute refer to as your 'signature strengths'. You can introduce team and individual activities to develop those strengths further; for some ideas, take a look at the

---

1   www.viacharacter.org

book by me and Elizabeth Wright: *Character Toolkit for Teachers* (Roberts and Wright 2018).

▮ OVER TO YOU

1. Reflect on and write down your top five character strengths. These could be the ones you feel most comfortable using, or you find yourself using most frequently, or even the ones that give you the most energy. You may also want to take the free VIA strengths survey[2] to find out which of their 24 character strengths come out as your strongest ones.

2. Consider and write down the strengths you regularly bring to your school. Which ones would you like to use more in your work?

3. Now reflect on the key strengths you see in the team around you within the school community. If there are particular strengths you would like to develop further, consider how you can do this – for example, by organizing conferences, training sessions, information evenings, building them into the school curriculum, etc. Write down your ideas.

What do you dream of?

Finally, I asked people I interviewed to dream as big as they could – for their school and for education.

By far the biggest category of responses, accounting for nearly one-third of all answers, can be summarized as 'every school, every child'.

I'd like to see more co-operation between state and private schools, comprehensive and grammar schools. Well-being, Positive Education, Character Education is something that can bind those schools together – young people are young people, they face the

---

2   www.viacharacter.org/survey/account/register

same fundamental challenges. Our system is quite divided; I would like to see bridges built across the UK education system. Well-being and character is the glue that can bind and create this collaboration.

Fabian de Fabiani

A big sub-theme here was about how schools are measured and judged, nationally and internationally. Comparisons based on academic achievement are seen as detrimental. Teacher training was one of the aspects raised. Teachers should be taught about Positive Psychology and Character Education, so they can apply that knowledge in their own lives and with the children they teach. There was much generosity in the answers I received, too. Teachers who are doing and seeing amazing Positive Education initiatives and outcomes in their schools want to share what they know with other teachers and other schools, so that it becomes available to all children.

The next biggest response category, with around 10 percent of responses, was that we (society and school leaders) need to value teachers more so that we attract and retain the best, as our children deserve nothing less.

Children are the future and teachers are being driven out. If it's not seen as a respected profession, we can't achieve anything.

Claire Probert

We should talk up education more. It's the career that makes other careers.

Patrick Ottley-O'Connor

Also with around 10 percent of responses was the category best summarized as 'equipping children for the future'. Educators want children to learn to make the right decisions and they want children to be equipped with the skills and character strengths for the future.

The education system should work with futurists. 'What skills will this 3-year-old need in 20 years' time?'

Katrina Mankani

Courageous leadership also ranked highly amongst the responses. Leaders want other leaders to be brave and go on this journey with them, to focus on flourishing as an objective for education, to remain true to their beliefs rather than bow to the pressures of inspections, to deliver what they know the children need, not what they are told to deliver.

Funding was also brought up by a few contributors: more funding for early interventions in school and from external agencies, for school counsellors, psychologists and other specialists, and to bring in external providers to inspire, train and consult so that schools can better help children (and adults) flourish.

■ OVER TO YOU

1. If there were no restrictions on financial and other resources, and anything was possible, what would your three dreams be for your school? For education? Write down your answers.

2. What steps can you personally take to get closer to turning those dreams into reality? Write them down.

The future of education is in your extremely capable hands. You've got this! Together, we can and we will do better for our children and for all those wonderful human beings who dedicate their lives to educating them.

So, for flourishing's sake, take the first step, however small, and join hands with the millions of other educators taking small steps! Together, we are unstoppable!

Appendix

The Roots of the 'LeAF' Tree

The roots of the tree in the LeAF model (Roberts 2019), as shown in Figure 1.1. in the Introduction, represent the elements of Positive Psychology and character strengths that underpin Positive Education. These are:

- Character strengths, virtues and values (The Jubilee Centre for Character and Virtues 2017; Peterson and Seligman 2004; Seligman *et al.* 2005).

- PERMA – positive emotion, engagement, relationships, meaning and accomplishments (Seligman 2012).

- 10 keys to happier living (Action for Happiness n.d.).

- Broaden-and-build theory of positive emotions (Fredrickson 2004).

- Emotional granularity (Tugade, Fredrickson and Barrett 2004).

- 'Mental Contrasting' (Oettingen *et al.* 2015).

- 'Growth Mindset' (Dweck 2006).

- Social and emotional learning has been referenced extensively in research into Character Education by Berkowitz and Bier (2005), and elements of it are referred to in the Programme for International Student Assessment (PISA) well-being infographic (OECD 2015).

- The culture root relates to supporting children's sense of cultural identity and belonging (Unicef 1989) and their ability to enjoy cultural activities, events and opportunities, including but not limited to the arts, music and sport (Ofsted 2019a).

References

Action for Happiness (n.d.) *10 keys to happier living*. Accessed on 15/09/19 at www.actionforhappiness.org/10-keys

Adler, A. (2016) 'Teaching well-being increases academic performance: Evidence from Bhutan, Mexico, and Peru.' University of Pennsylvania. Accessed on 15/09/19 at https://repository.upenn.edu/edissertations/1572

AI Commons (n.d.) *5-D Cycle of Appreciative Inquiry*. Accessed on 15/09/19 at https://appreciativeinquiry.champlain.edu/learn/appreciative-inquiry-introduction/5-d-cycle-appreciative-inquiry

Arthur, J., Kristjánsson, K., Walker, D., Sanderse, W. *et al.* (2015) *Character Education in UK schools: Research report*. Accessed on 15/09/19 at www.jubileecentre.ac.uk/userfiles/jubileecentre/pdf/Research Reports/Character_Education_in_UK_Schools.pdf

Bates, A. J. (2019) *Finnish Education: Balance for Better – Part 3*. Accessed on 15/09/19 at https://adelebateseducation.co.uk/finnish-education-balance-for-better-part-3

Berkowitz, M. W. and Bier, M. C. (2005) 'What works in Character Education : A research-driven guide for educators Character Education Partnership.' *Education*, February, 1–37.

Boniwell, I. (2018) *Slide presented during a lecture as part of the MSc in Applied Positive Psychology at Anglia Ruskin University in Paris on 19th February 2018*. Accessed on 15/09/19 at http://aps.sg/files/GELC 2014/Keynote Slides/Dr_Boniwell_-_Singapore_Leadership_Conference_Read-Only.pdf

Cooperrider, D. L., Whitney, D. K. and Stavros, J. M. (2003) *Appreciative Inquiry Handbook: The First in a Series of AI Workbooks for Leaders of Change (Vol. 1)*. Oakland, CA: Berrett-Koehler Publishers.

Department Determinants of Health and Wellbeing, Directorate of Health in Iceland (2018) 'Health Promoting Schools in Health Promoting Communities.' Unpublished document (PowerPoint slides) obtained from Dóra Guðrún Guðmundsdóttir.

Department for Children, Schools and Families (2008) *Targeted mental health in schools project: Using the evidence to inform your approach: A practical guide for headteachers and commissioners*. Department for Children, Schools and Families. Accessed on 15/09/19 at https://dera.ioe.ac.uk/28416/1/00784-2008bkt-en.pdf

Department for Education (2017) *Developing character skills in schools: Summary report*. Department for Education. Accessed on 15/09/19 at www.gov.uk/government/publications/developing-character-skills-in-schools

Durlak, J. A., Weissberg, R. P., Dymnicki, A. B., Taylor, R. D. and Schellinger, K. B. (2011) 'The impact of enhancing students' social and emotional learning: A meta-analysis of school-based universal interventions.' *Child Development 82*, 1, 405–432.

Dweck, C. S. (2006) *Mindset: The New Psychology of Success*. New York, NY: Random House Incorporated.

Education Support Partnership (2018) *Teacher Wellbeing Index 2018*. London: Education Support Partnership. Accessed on15/09/19 at www.educationsupportpartnership.org.uk/sites/default/files/teacher_wellbeing_index_2018.pdf

Elfrink, T. R., Goldberg, J. M., Schreurs, K. M. G., Bohlmeijer, E. T. and Clarke, A. M. (2017) 'Positive educative programme: A whole school approach to supporting children's wellbeing and creating a positive school climate: A pilot study.' *Health Education 117*, 2, 215–230.

Fredrickson, B. L. (2004) 'Broaden-and-Build Theory of Positive Emotions.' *The Royal Society 359*, 1449, 1367–1377.

Frith, E. (2016) *CentreForum Commission on Children and Young People's Mental Health: State of the Nation*. Accessed on 15/09/19 at www.crisiscareconcordat.org.uk/inspiration/centreforum-commission-children-young-peoples-mental-health-state-nation-april-2016

Hammond, S. A. (2013) *The Thin Book of Appreciative Inquiry*. Bend, OR: Thin Book Publishing.

Hoare, E., Bott, D. and Robinson, J. (2017) 'Learn it, Live it, Teach it, Embed it: Implementing a whole school approach to foster positive mental health and wellbeing through Positive Education.' *International Journal of Wellbeing 7*, 3, 56–71.

Humphrey, N., Lendrum, A. and Wigelsworth, M. (2010) *Social and emotional aspects of learning (SEAL) programme in secondary schools: National evaluation*. Department for Education. Accessed on 15/09/19 at www.gov.uk/government/publications/social-and-emotional-aspects-of-learning-seal-programme-in-secondary-schools-national-evaluation

Johnson, B., Down, B., Le Cornu, R., Peters, J. *et al.* (2014) 'Promoting early career teacher resilience: A framework for understanding and acting.' *Teachers and Teaching: Theory and Practice 20*, 5, 530–546.

Jubilee Centre for Character and Virtues (n.d.-a) *Character caught: School ethos self-evaluation framework*. Birmingham: The Jubilee Centre for Character & Virtues. Accessed on 08/01/20 at https://www.jubileecentre.ac.uk/userfiles/jubileecentre/pdf/character-education/EvaluationHandbook/Section2_CharacterCaught.pdf

Jubilee Centre for Character and Virtues (n.d.-b) *Character education: Evaluation handbook for schools - section 1 - planning & evaluation*. Birmingham: The Jubilee Centre for Character & Virtues. Accessed on 08/01/20 at https://www.jubileecentre.ac.uk/userfiles/jubileecentre/pdf/character-education/EvaluationHandbook/Section1_PlanningAnEvaluation.pdf

Jubilee Centre for Character and Virtues (n.d.-c) *Schools of character*. Birmingham: The Jubilee Centre for Character & Virtues. Accessed on 15/09/19 at www.jubileecentre.ac.uk/userfiles/jubileecentre/pdf/character-education/SchoolsOfCharacterPDF.pdf

Jubilee Centre for Character and Virtues (n.d.-d) *Character taught: Perspectives on evaluating curriculum strategies and activities*. Birmingham: The Jubilee Centre for Character & Virtues. Accessed on 08/01/20 at https://www.jubileecentre.ac.uk/userfiles/jubileecentre/pdf/character-education/EvaluationHandbook/Section3_CharacterTaught.pdf

Jubilee Centre for Character and Virtues (2017) *A Framework for Character Education in Schools*. Birmingham: The Jubilee Centre for Character & Virtues. Accessed 08/01/20 at https://www.jubileecentre.ac.uk/userfiles/jubileecentre/pdf/character-education/Framework%20for%20Character%20Education.pdf

Konu, A. and Rimpelä, M. (2002) 'Well-being in schools: A conceptual model.' *Health Promotion International 17*, 1, 79–87.

Kristjánsson, K. (2012) 'Positive Psychology and Positive Education: Old wine in new bottles?' *Educational Psychologist 47*, 2, 86–105.

Lopes, J., Oliveira, C., Reed, L. and Gable, R. A. (2013) 'Character Education in Portugal.' *Childhood Education 89*, 5, 286–289.

Meiklejohn, J., Phillips, C., Freedman, M. L., Griffin, M. L. *et al.* (2012) 'Integrating mindfulness training into K-12 Education: Fostering the resilience of teachers and students.' *Mindfulness 3*, 4, 291–307.

Milson, A. J. (2000) 'Creating a curriculum for character development: A case study.' *The Clearing House 74*, 2, 89–93.

Ministry of Education, Science and Culture with the Directorate of Health, Iceland (n.d.) 'The Icelandic National Curriculum Guides and Health Promoting Schools, synergy with inter-sectoral cooperation.' Unpublished document obtained from Dóra Guðrún Guðmundsdóttir.

Moffat, A. (2017) *No Outsiders in Our School: Teaching the Equality Act in Primary Schools* (Speechmark Practical Resources). Abingdon: Routledge. (Recommended by Rebecca Tigue.)

Morgan, N. (2017) *Taught Not Caught: Educating for 21st Century Character.* Woodbridge: John Catt Educational Limited.

Morris, I. (2012) 'Going beyond the Accidental: Happiness, Education, and the Wellington College Experience.' In S. David, I. Boniwell and A. Conley Ayers (eds) *Oxford Handbook of Happiness.* Oxford: Oxford University Press.

Morris, I. (2015) *Teaching Happiness and Well-Being in Schools: Learning to Ride Elephants.* London: Bloomsbury Publishing.

NatCen (2017) *Developing character skills in schools: Summary report.* Department for Education. Accessed on 16/09/19 at www.gov.uk/government/publications/developing-character-skills-in-schools

National Union of Teachers (2013) *Teacher Stress: NUT guidance to divisions and associations.* NUT. Accessed on 16/09/19 at www.teachers.org.uk/files/TACKLING-STRESS-0713.doc

Noble, T. (2017) 'Positive education at the cross roads: Important sign points for going in the right direction.' In M. A. White, G. R. Slemp and A. S. Murray (eds) *Future Directions in Well-Being: Education, Organizations and Policy.* Dordrecht: Springer.

Norrish, J. M. (2015) *Positive Education: The Geelong Grammar School Journey.* Oxford Positive Psychology Series. Oxford: Oxford University Press.

OECD (n.d.) *Programme for International Student Assessment (PISA).* Accessed on 16/09/19 at www.oecd.org/pisa

OECD (2015) *PISA well-being infographics.* Accessed on 16/09/19 at www.oecd.org/education/pisa-2015-results-volume-iii-9789264273856-en.htm

Oettingen, G., Kappes, H. B., Guttenburg, K. B. and Gollwitzer, P. M. (2015) 'Self-regulation of time management: Mental contrasting with implementation intentions.' *European Journal of Social Psychology 45*, 218–229.

Ofsted (2019a) *School Inspection Handbook. Draft for consultation.* Ofsted. Accessed on 16/09/19 at https://assets.publishing.service.gov.uk/government/uploads/system/uploads/attachment_data/file/772065/Schools_draft_handbook_180119.pdf

Ofsted (2019b) *The education inspection framework. Draft for consultation.* Ofsted. Accessed on 03/06/19 at www.gov.uk/government/publications/education-inspection-framework-draft-for-consultation

Patel, V., Flisher, A. J., Hetrick, S. and McGorry, P. (2007) 'Mental health of young people: A global public-health challenge.' *Lancet 369*, 9569, 1302–1313.

Payne, A. A. (2018) *Creating and sustaining a positive and communal school climate: Contemporary research, present obstacles, and future directions.* U.S. Department of Justice. Accessed on 16/09/19 at www.ncjrs.gov/pdffiles1/nij/250209.pdf

Peterson, C. and Seligman, M. E. P. (2004) *Character Strengths and Virtues.* Oxford: Oxford University Press.

Public Health England (2014) *The link between pupil health and wellbeing and attainment.* Public Health England. Accessed on 16/09/19 at https://assets.publishing.service.gov.uk/government/uploads/system/uploads/attachment_data/file/370686/HT_briefing_layoutvFINALvii.pdf

Public Health England (2015) *Promoting children and young people's emotional health and wellbeing: A whole school and college approach.* Accessed on 16/09/19 at www.gov.uk/government/uploads/system/uploads/attachment_data/file/414908/Final_EHWB_draft_20_03_15.pdf

Roberts, F. (2018) 'Whole school positive education in the United Kingdom.' Unpublished manuscript, Anglia Ruskin University. Available on request from fred@happiness-speaker.co.uk

Roberts, F. (2019) 'LeAF: The Learn and Flourish Model and Self-Evaluation Framework for Whole School Positive Education.' Unpublished manuscript, Anglia Ruskin University. Available on request from fred@happiness-speaker.co.uk

Roberts, F. and Wright, E. (2018) *Character Toolkit for Teachers. 100+ Classroom and Whole School Character Education Activities for 5- to 11-Year-Olds.* London: Jessica Kingsley Publishers.

Roffey, S. (2012) 'Developing Positive Relationships in Schools.' In S. Roffey (ed.) *Positive Relationships: Evidence Based Practice across the World.* Berlin/Heidelberg: Springer Science + Business Media.

Seligman, M. E. P. (2012) *Flourish: A Visionary New Understanding of Happiness and Well-Being.* New York, NY: Simon and Schuster.

Seligman, M. E. P., Adler, A., Al Karam, A., Peng, K. P., Seldon, A. and Waters, L. (2018) 'Positive Education.' In *Global Happiness Policy Report.* Global Happiness Council (GHC). Accessed on 16/09/19 at https://s3.amazonaws.com/ghc-2018/GlobalHappinessPolicyReport2018.pdf

Seligman, M. E. P., Adler, A., Al Karam, A., Peng, K. P., Seldon, A. and Waters, L. (2019) 'Positive Education.' In *Global Happiness and Well-Being Policy Report.* Global Happiness Council (GHC). Accessed on 16/09/19 at https://s3.amazonaws.com/ghwbpr-2019/UAE/GH19_Ch4.pdf

Seligman, M. E. P. and Csikszentmihalyi, M. (2000) 'Positive psychology: An introduction.' *American Psychologist 55,* 1, 5–14.

Seligman, M. E. P., Ernst, R. M., Gillham, J., Reivich, K. and Linkins, M. (2009) 'Positive education: Positive psychology and classroom interventions.' *Oxford Review of Education 35,* 3, 293–311.

Seligman, M. E. P., Steen, T. A., Park, N. and Peterson, C. (2005) 'Positive psychology progress: Empirical validation of interventions.' *American Psychologist 60,* 410–421.

Sergiovanni, T. J. (1994) *Building Community in Schools.* San Francisco, CA: Jossey-Bass.

Shankland, R. and Rosset, E. (2017) 'Review of brief school-based positive psychological interventions: A taster for teachers and educators.' *Educational Psychology Review 29,* 363–392.

Shoshani, A., Steinmetz, S. and Kanat-Maymon, Y. (2016) 'Effects of the Maytiv positive psychology school program on early adolescents' well-being, engagement, and achievement.' *Journal of School Psychology 57,* 73–92.

Srivastava, S. and Cooperrider, D. (1990) *Appreciative Inquiry and Leadership: The Power of Positive Thought and Action in Organizations.* San Francisco, CA: Jossey-Bass.

Stirling, S. and Emery, H. (2016) *A whole school framework for emotional well-being and mental health: Supporting resources for school leaders.* National Children's Bureau. Accessed on 16/09/19 at www.ncb.org.uk/sites/default/files/field/attachment/NCB School Well Being Framework Leaders Resources FINAL.pdf

Stixrud, W. (2019) *The Self-Driven Child: The Science and Sense of Giving Your Kids More Control over Their Lives.* London: Penguin Books.

Thomson, P. (2010) *Whole School Change: A Literature Review (2nd edn).* Creativity, Culture and Education series. Accessed on 16/09/19 at http://old.creativitycultureeducation.org/wp-content/uploads/cce-lit-review-whole-school-change-255.pdf

Tough, P. (2013) *How Children Succeed: Grit, Curiosity, and the Hidden Power of Character.* London: Random House Books.

Townley Grammar School (n.d.) *Character Education at Townley Grammar School.* Bexleyheath: Townley Grammar School.

Tugade, M. M., Fredrickson, B. L. and Barrett, L. F. (2004) 'Psychological resilience and positive emotional granularity: Examining the benefits of positive emotions on coping and health.' *Journal of Personality 72,* 6, 1161–1190.

Unicef (1989) *The United Nations Convention on the Rights of the Child.* Unicef. Accessed on 16/09/19 at www.unicef.org.uk/what-we-do/un-convention-child-rights

Waters, L. (2011) 'A review of school-based positive psychology interventions.' *Australian Educational and Developmental Psychologist 28,* 2, 75–90.

Waters, L. (2014) 'Balancing the curriculum: Teaching gratitude, hope and resilience.' In H. Sykes (ed.) *A Love of Ideas.* Melbourne: Future Leaders.

Waters, L. (2017) 'Visible wellbeing in schools: The powerful role of instructional leadership.' *Australian Educational Leader 39*, 1, 6.

Waters, L., White, M. A., Wang, L. and Murray, A. S. (2015) 'Leading whole-school change.' In M. A. White and A. S. Murray (eds) *Evidence-Based Approaches in Positive Education.* Dordrecht: Springer.

Weare, K. (2015) *What works in promoting social and emotional well-being and responding to mental health problems in schools? Advice for schools and framework document.* National Children's Bureau. Accessed on 16/09/19 at www.mentalhealth.org.nz/assets/ResourceFinder/What-works-in-promoting-social-and-emotional-wellbeing-in-schools-2015.pdf

Weare, K. and Markham, W. (2005) 'What do we know about promoting mental health through schools?' *Promotion and Education 12*, 3–4, 118–122. https://doi.org/10.1177/10253823050120030104

Westheimer, J. and Kahne, J. (2004) 'Educating the "good" citizen: Political choices and pedagogical goals.' *PS – Political Science and Politics 37*, 2, 241–247.

White, M. A. (2016) 'Why won't it stick? Positive Psychology and Positive Education.' *Psychology of Well-Being 6*, 1, 2.

White, M. A. and Murray, A. S. (2015) 'Building a positive institution.' In M. A. White and A. S. Murray (eds) *Evidence-Based Approaches in Positive Education.* Dordrecht: Springer.

White, R. and Warfa, N. (2011) 'Building schools of character: A case-study investigation of character education's impact on school climate, pupil behavior, and curriculum delivery.' *Journal of Applied Social Psychology 41*, 1, 45–60.

World Government Summit (2017) *The state of positive education.* World Government Summit in collaboration with IPEN. Accessed on 16/09/19 at www.worldgovernmentsummit.org/api/publications/document/8f647dc4-e97c-6578-b2f8-ff0000a7ddb6

Further Reading

Bethune, A. (2018) *Wellbeing in the Primary Classroom: A Practical Guide to Teaching Happiness*. London: Bloomsbury Education.

Boniwell, I. and Ryan, L. (2012) *Personal Well-Being Lessons for Secondary Schools: Positive Psychology in Action for 11 to 14 year olds*. Maidenhead: Open University Press.

Cowley, A. (2019) *The Wellbeing Toolkit: Sustaining, Supporting and Enabling School Staff*. London: Bloomsbury Education.

Crehan, L. (2018) *Cleverlands: The Secrets behind the Success of the World's Education Superpowers*. London: Unbound. (Recommended by Adele Bates.)

Larivvee, B. (2012) *Cultivating Teacher Renewal: Guarding Against Stress and Burnout*. Plymouth: Rowman and Littlefield Education. (Recommended by Ian Flintoff.)

MacConville, R. and Rae, T. (2012) *Building Happiness, Resilience and Motivation in Adolescents: A Positive Psychology Curriculum for Well-Being*. London: Jessica Kingsley Publishers.

Moffat, A. (2017) *No Outsiders in Our School: Teaching the Equality Act in Primary Schools* (Speechmark Practical Resources). Abingdon: Routledge. (Recommended by Rebecca Tigue.)

Morgan, N. (2017) *Taught Not Caught: Educating for 21st Century Character*. Woodbridge: John Catt Educational Limited.

Pardoe, D. (2009) *Towards Successful Learning (2nd edn)*. London and New York: Continuum International Publishing Group. (Recommended by Flora Barton.)

Roberts, F. and Wright, E. (2018) *Character Toolkit for Teachers. 100+ Classroom and Whole School Character Education Activities for 5- to 11-Year-Olds*. London: Jessica Kingsley Publishers.

Sahlberg, P. (2014) *Finnish Lessons 2.0: What Can the World Learn from Educational Change in Finland?* New York: Teachers College Press. (Recommended by Adele Bates.)

Stixrud, W. (2019) *The Self-Driven Child: The Science and Sense of Giving Your Kids More Control over Their Lives*. London: Penguin Books. (Recommended by Rebecca Comizio.)

Other JKP titles

Character Toolkit for Teachers
100+ Classroom and Whole School Character
Education Activities for 5- to 11-Year-Olds
Frederika Roberts and Elizabeth Wright
Foreword by Kristján Kristjánsson

£16.99 | $24.95 | PB | 184PP | ISBN: 978 1 78592 490 3 |
eISBN: 978 1 78450 879 1

This accessible and much-needed resource sets out advice on how to develop character and encourage well-being in pupils aged 5–11.

Schools are increasingly aware of how beneficial positive character skills can be, but resources on how to develop them are scarce. This book gives teachers the means to promote gratitude, positive emotions, character strengths and positive relationships through 100+ easy-to-implement activities such as student diaries, classroom displays and letter writing campaigns. It also includes tools and strategies that go beyond the classroom, helping to embed Character Education into the culture and ethos of the entire school. Each chapter will include a short introduction to the relevant theoretical background, and all activities are based on validated Character Education and positive psychology interventions.

Bite-sized and practical, and full of ideas that can be dipped in and out of in the classroom, this is an ideal book for busy teachers.

Character Toolkit Strength Cards
Frederika Roberts and Elizabeth Wright
Illustrated by David O'Connell

£18.99 | $27.95 | Card set | ISBN: 978 1 78775 273 3 | 32pp| 30 cards |

Growing up presents many challenges and positive learning experiences. Helping young people understand, name and talk about their and other peoples' strengths can improve their relationships with their friends, family and the wider community.

The interactive *Character Toolkit Strength Cards* enable children to learn, recognise and express all sides of their character. The cards promote character strengths such as perseverance, grit and leadership alongside moral and civic strengths such as gratitude and kindness.

These cards have been designed to allow teachers, parents and counsellors in coaching settings to explore all character strength within children. Included is a booklet of different activities that provide suggestions for using the strength cards. These include activities that encourage children to describe the strength they are most proud of, or how to identify strengths in others around them.

These positive, helpful and authentic strength cards will be a useful classroom resource, focusing on encouraging the next generation to be their best self.

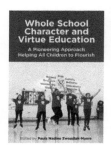

Whole School Character and Virtue Education
A Pioneering Approach Helping All Children to Flourish
Edited by Paula Nadine Zwozdiak-Myers

£19.99 | $29.95 | PB | 192PP | ISBN: 978 1 78592 875 8 | eISBN: 978 1 78592 874 1

Using the successful implementation achieved at Yeading Junior School, this book provides strategies and advice about how to widely implement Character Education in schools. This helpful guide answers the following questions schools and teachers have when considering how to develop Character Education:

- What character virtues are important in primary education?

- How can these be cultivated within the formal and informal curricula?

- How do we know if strategies are working and successful?

- What constitutes evidence of best practice?

With contributions from professional practitioners ranging from building partnerships in the community, intergenerational learning, using character virtues in work with vulnerable children and children with SEND, financial literacy and the diverse religious context of primary education, the book explores the opportunities for developing character virtues and virtue literacy with the purpose of supporting pupils to flourish in society. With the help of this book, schools can create an environment and ethos where learners are not only successful but can make a real difference to the world.